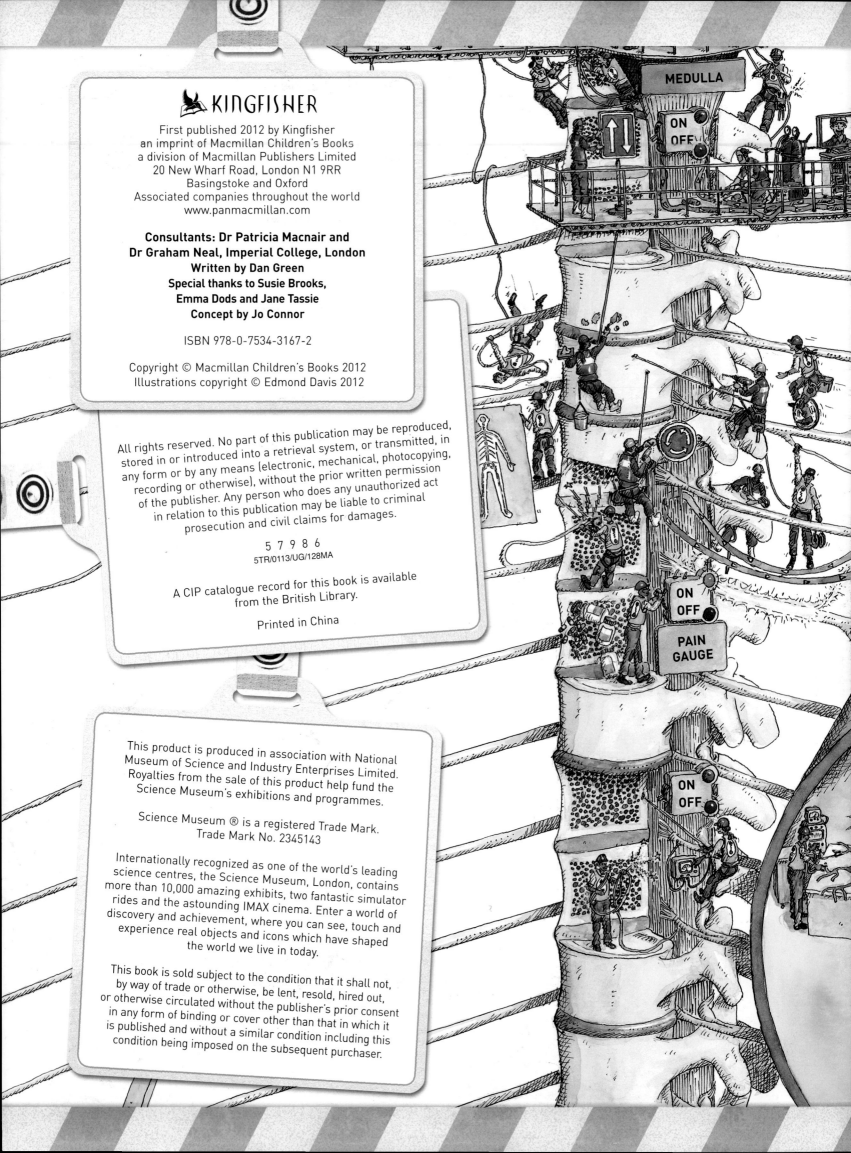

KINGFISHER

First published 2012 by Kingfisher
an imprint of Macmillan Children's Books
a division of Macmillan Publishers Limited
20 New Wharf Road, London N1 9RR
Basingstoke and Oxford
Associated companies throughout the world
www.panmacmillan.com

**Consultants: Dr Patricia Macnair and
Dr Graham Neal, Imperial College, London
Written by Dan Green
Special thanks to Susie Brooks,
Emma Dods and Jane Tassie
Concept by Jo Connor**

ISBN 978-0-7534-3167-2

Copyright © Macmillan Children's Books 2012
Illustrations copyright © Edmond Davis 2012

This product is produced in association with National Museum of Science and Industry Enterprises Limited. Royalties from the sale of this product help fund the Science Museum's exhibitions and programmes.

Science Museum ® is a registered Trade Mark. Trade Mark No. 2345143

Internationally recognized as one of the world's leading science centres, the Science Museum, London, contains more than 10,000 amazing exhibits, two fantastic simulator rides and the astounding IMAX cinema. Enter a world of discovery and achievement, where you can see, touch and experience real objects and icons which have shaped the world we live in today.

MEDULLA

ON
OFF

ON
OFF

PAIN
GAUGE

ON
OFF

Contents

Don't forget to inspect the amazing Human Body Factory poster!

YOU ARE HERE

Welcome to the Human Body Factory! You're about to take a wild rollercoaster tour of the cranking, sloshing, pumping parts that keep you alive and kicking! Discover each bit of your body as a busy department, packed with wacky workers and manic machines. To check where you are in the body, look for the red dot on a figure like this in the introduction tag.

The **respiratory system** draws oxygen into the body and gets rid of carbon dioxide gas. Air shoots in through the mouth or nose and continues to the **lungs**, which pass the oxygen over to the blood.

Each division of the Human Body Factory works non-stop to do its job – there's no chance of a holiday around here! The different departments clunk and churn in their own ways, but they all need each other to keep the body healthy. They come together in **ten major body systems**.

The **immune system** keeps the works healthy and infection-free, using killer cells and chemical weapons. It's given a helping hand by the **skin, hair and nails**, which wrap the body in a protective casing. Meanwhile, the **endocrine system** monitors how body cells work and change, affecting how fast we burn energy and how we grow and develop.

IMMUNE CELLS

 Neutrophil Blasts bacteria and fungi

 Eosinophil Targets larger parasites and activates allergic response

 Basophil Triggers allergic response

 Monocyte Mops up dead cells

 T-cell Fights viruses and cancer cells

 B-cell Memorizes ways of making antibodies

 Mast cell General protection close to the skin

The **cardiovascular system** sends **blood** to all parts of the body, using the **heart** to pump it around. The blood takes deliveries to all the body's cells, and carries away their waste including taking carbon dioxide to the lungs.

The **mouth**, **stomach** and **intestines** mush up food in the **digestive system**. With a bit of help from the **liver**, they get at the good bits and circulate them in the blood. Any leftovers leave the body as poo.

Waste that builds up in the blood is filtered by the **kidneys** and turned into pee by the **urinary system**. It gets stored for a while in the **bladder** before leaving the body for good.

EXIT

The **reproductive system** manages the planning and construction of new human units.

So are you ready to shoot down arteries and squelch around the stomach? Look out for the gnashing, grinding mouth – and don't get stuck in the bogeys at the nose station! Along the way, keep a sharp eye out for Clatterbones, the skeleton. He's hiding throughout the book, and you can award yourself a brain cell each time you spot him!

HEAD OFFICE

The **nervous system** is led by head office – the **brain**. It monitors what's going on inside and outside of the body, and sends messages along the **nerves** to operate the **musculoskeletal system** so that the body can move.

COME ON THEN, LET'S NOT WAIT ANY LONGER...

The Brain

The Human Body Factory would be chaos without its head office, the brain! This bossy department controls all the body's movements and also generates thoughts, dreams, memories and problem-solving powers. It works using nerve cells called neurons, which zap signals between each other at lightning speed.

YOU ARE HERE

Thalamus
Hypo-thalamus
Olfactory bulb (smell)
Cerebral cortex
Hippo-campus
Amygdala
Cerebellum

The outer layer of the brain is the **cerebral cortex**. It looks like a wrinkly walnut, but there are other parts hidden inside!

Come on **thalamus** team – let's get these sense signals from the nervous system to the right parts of the brain.

It's the **neuron** cell bodies that do all the main brain work. They form an outer layer called **grey matter**. Underneath, in the **white matter**, fibres link the neurons together.

Feeling moody? Blame the **hypothalamus**. We work closely with the endocrine system (see pages 16–17).

Now where did I put those old memories? In the **hippocampus** we make sure the boss remembers things!

Each half, or **hemisphere**, of the brain handles slightly different tasks. One is always more bossy than the other. It dictates whether a person is left- or right-handed.

H-E-L-P! The **amygdala** is the area that holds our deepest fears.

Shh, I'm trying to concentrate! In the **reticular formation** we 'fade out' distractions. We also turn the brain off or on when it's time to sleep or wake up.

The brain guzzles up loads of energy and oxygen. We supply these in the blood, through a giant loop of **blood vessels**.

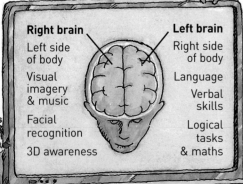

Right brain

Left side of body

Visual imagery & music

Facial recognition

3D awareness

Left brain

Right side of body

Language

Verbal skills

Logical tasks & maths

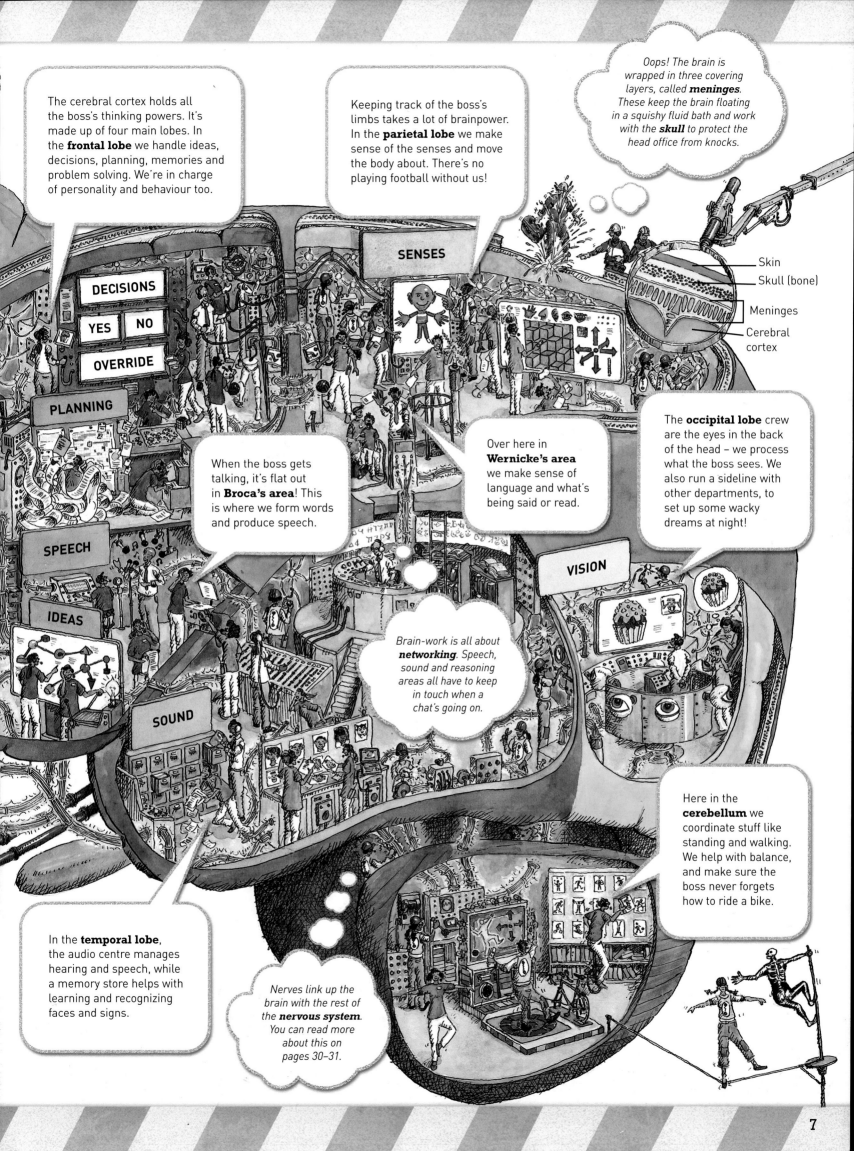

The cerebral cortex holds all the boss's thinking powers. It's made up of four main lobes. In the **frontal lobe** we handle ideas, decisions, planning, memories and problem solving. We're in charge of personality and behaviour too.

Keeping track of the boss's limbs takes a lot of brainpower. In the **parietal lobe** we make sense of the senses and move the body about. There's no playing football without us!

*Oops! The brain is wrapped in three covering layers, called **meninges**. These keep the brain floating in a squishy fluid bath and work with the **skull** to protect the head office from knocks.*

DECISIONS

YES NO

OVERRIDE

PLANNING

SENSES

Skin

Skull (bone)

Meninges

Cerebral cortex

SPEECH

When the boss gets talking, it's flat out in **Broca's area**! This is where we form words and produce speech.

Over here in **Wernicke's area** we make sense of language and what's being said or read.

The **occipital lobe** crew are the eyes in the back of the head – we process what the boss sees. We also run a sideline with other departments, to set up some wacky dreams at night!

IDEAS

VISION

SOUND

*Brain-work is all about **networking**. Speech, sound and reasoning areas all have to keep in touch when a chat's going on.*

Here in the **cerebellum** we coordinate stuff like standing and walking. We help with balance, and make sure the boss never forgets how to ride a bike.

In the **temporal lobe**, the audio centre manages hearing and speech, while a memory store helps with learning and recognizing faces and signs.

*Nerves link up the brain with the rest of the **nervous system**. You can read more about this on pages 30–31.*

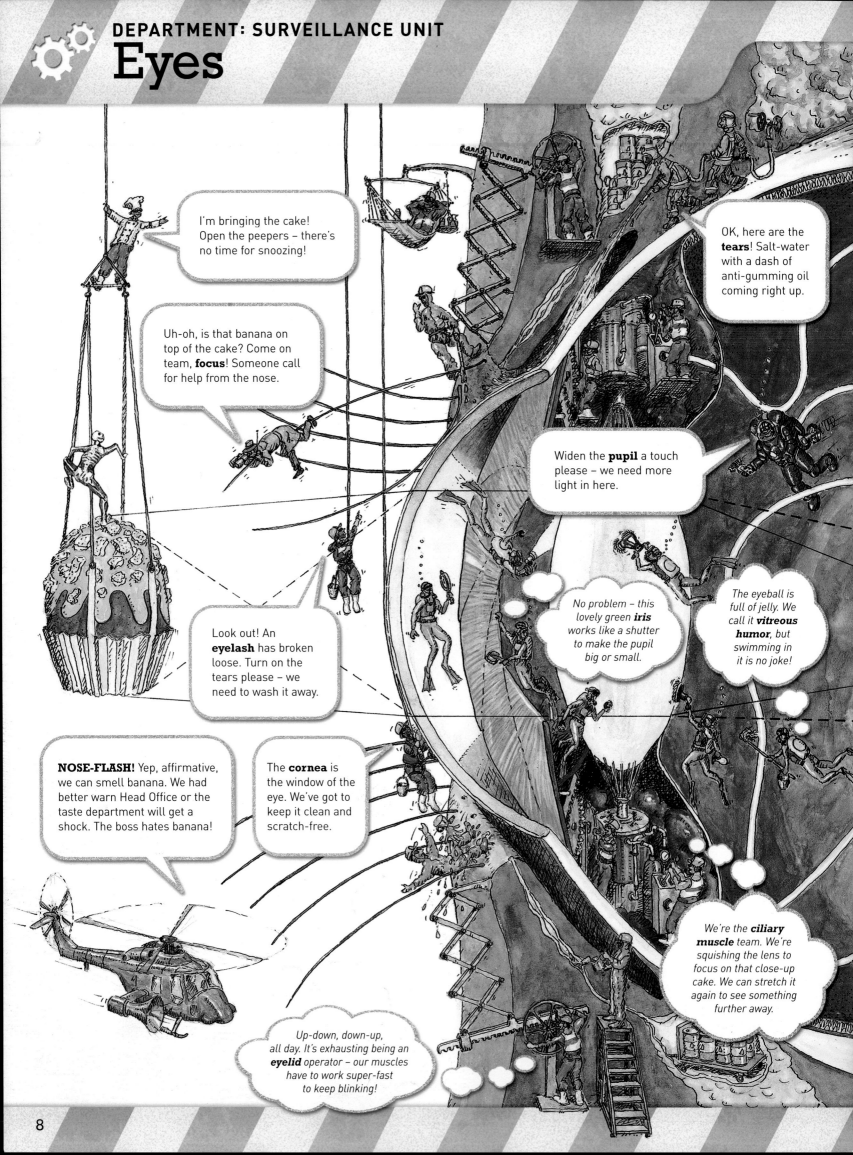

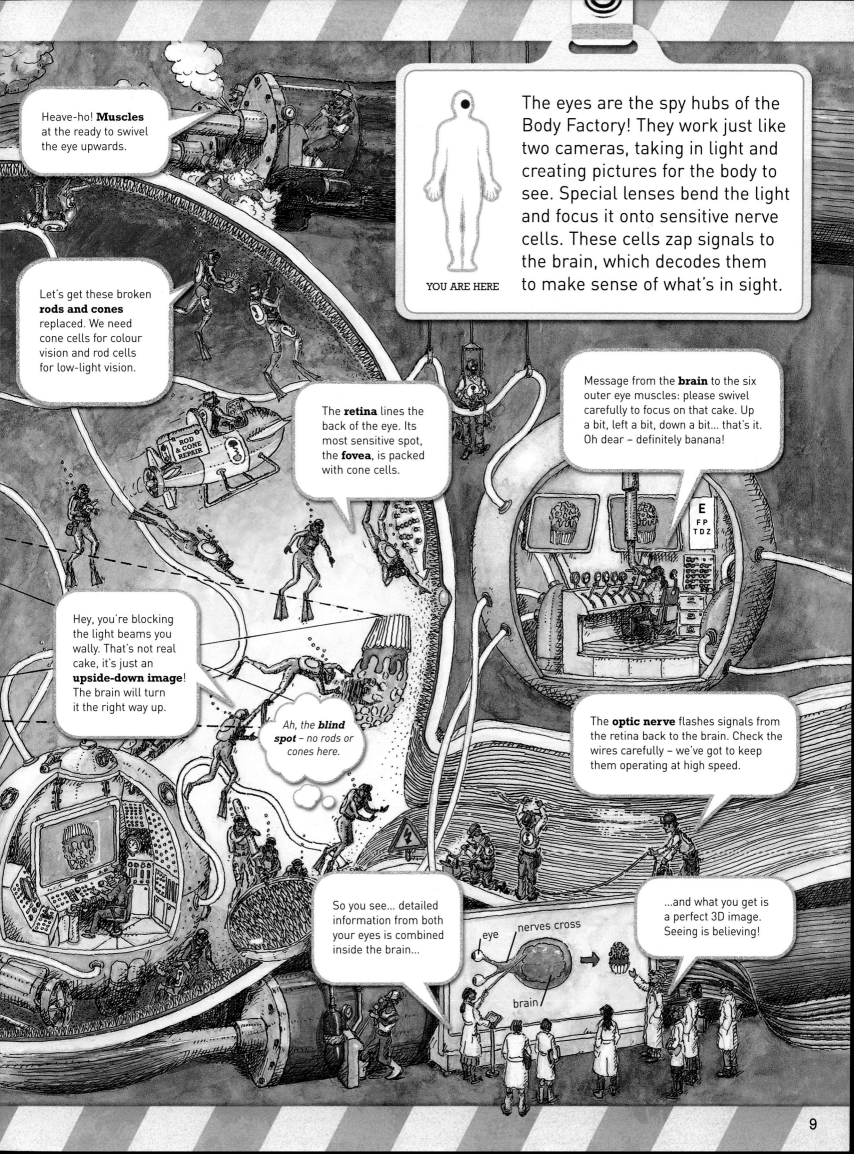

Ears

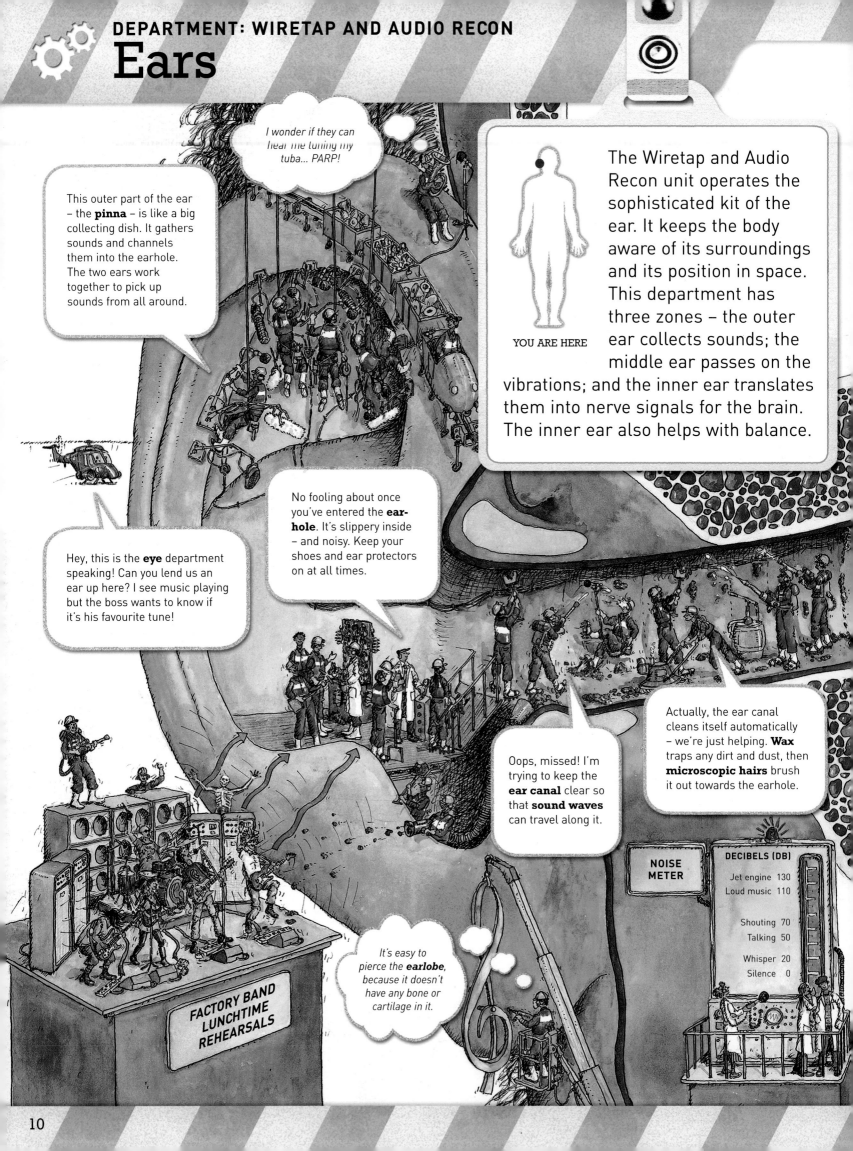

I wonder if they can hear me tuning my tuba... PARP!

This outer part of the ear – the **pinna** – is like a big collecting dish. It gathers sounds and channels them into the earhole. The two ears work together to pick up sounds from all around.

The Wiretap and Audio Recon unit operates the sophisticated kit of the ear. It keeps the body aware of its surroundings and its position in space. This department has three zones – the outer ear collects sounds; the middle ear passes on the vibrations; and the inner ear translates them into nerve signals for the brain. The inner ear also helps with balance.

YOU ARE HERE

Hey, this is the **eye** department speaking! Can you lend us an ear up here? I see music playing but the boss wants to know if it's his favourite tune!

No fooling about once you've entered the **ear-hole**. It's slippery inside – and noisy. Keep your shoes and ear protectors on at all times.

Actually, the ear canal cleans itself automatically – we're just helping. **Wax** traps any dirt and dust, then **microscopic hairs** brush it out towards the earhole.

Oops, missed! I'm trying to keep the **ear canal** clear so that **sound waves** can travel along it.

It's easy to pierce the **earlobe**, because it doesn't have any bone or cartilage in it.

FACTORY BAND LUNCHTIME REHEARSALS

NOISE METER	DECIBELS (DB)
	Jet engine 130
	Loud music 110
	Shouting 70
	Talking 50
	Whisper 20
	Silence 0

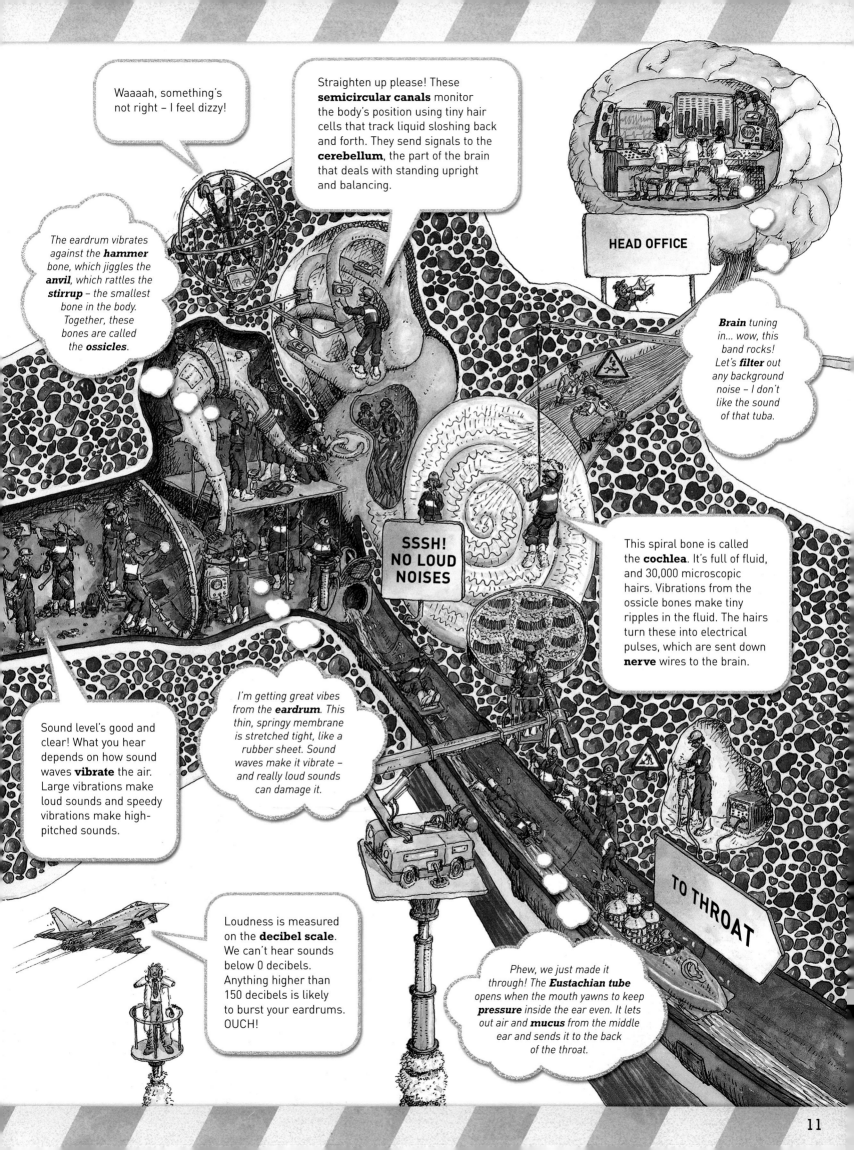

Nose

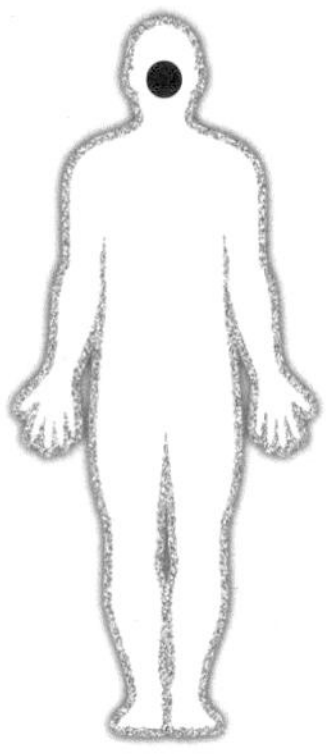

YOU ARE HERE

Welcome to the sniffy, whiffy smell-sense department! The nose is a slimy set of blowpipes that warms, moistens and cleans air on its way to the lungs. Deep inside is a small patch of nerve endings, which detect smell molecules in the air. The brain gets the message, then quickly works out what pongs.

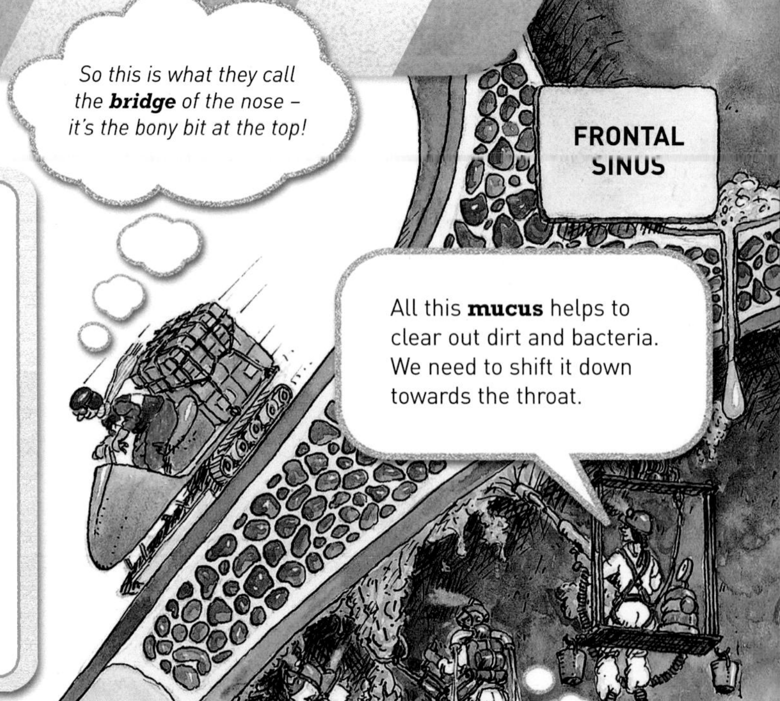

So this is what they call the **bridge** of the nose – it's the bony bit at the top!

FRONTAL SINUS

All this **mucus** helps to clear out dirt and bacteria. We need to shift it down towards the throat.

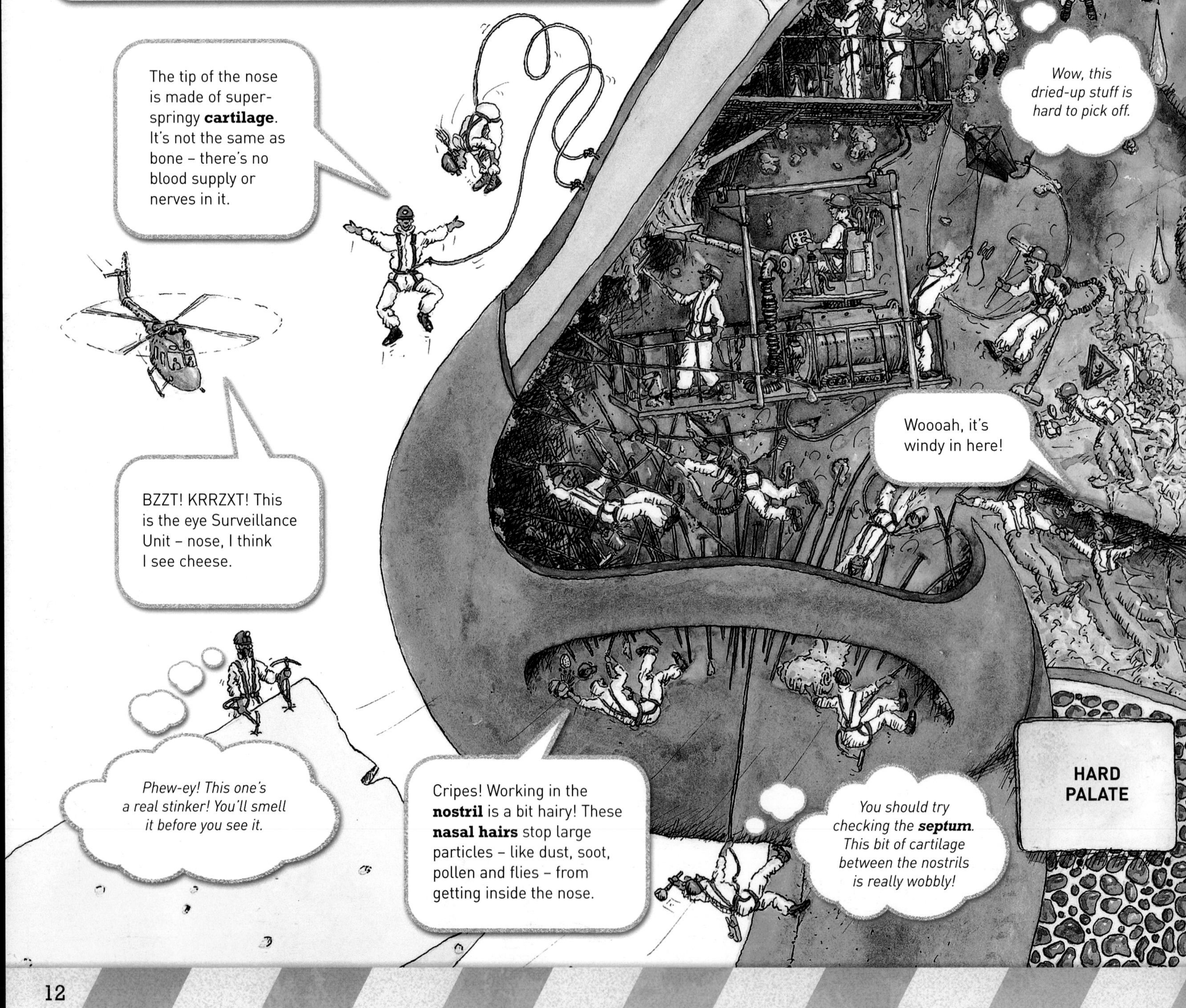

The tip of the nose is made of super-springy **cartilage**. It's not the same as bone – there's no blood supply or nerves in it.

Wow, this dried-up stuff is hard to pick off.

BZZT! KRRZXT! This is the eye Surveillance Unit – nose, I think I see cheese.

Woooah, it's windy in here!

Phew-ey! This one's a real stinker! You'll smell it before you see it.

Cripes! Working in the **nostril** is a bit hairy! These **nasal hairs** stop large particles – like dust, soot, pollen and flies – from getting inside the nose.

You should try checking the **septum**. This bit of cartilage between the nostrils is really wobbly!

HARD PALATE

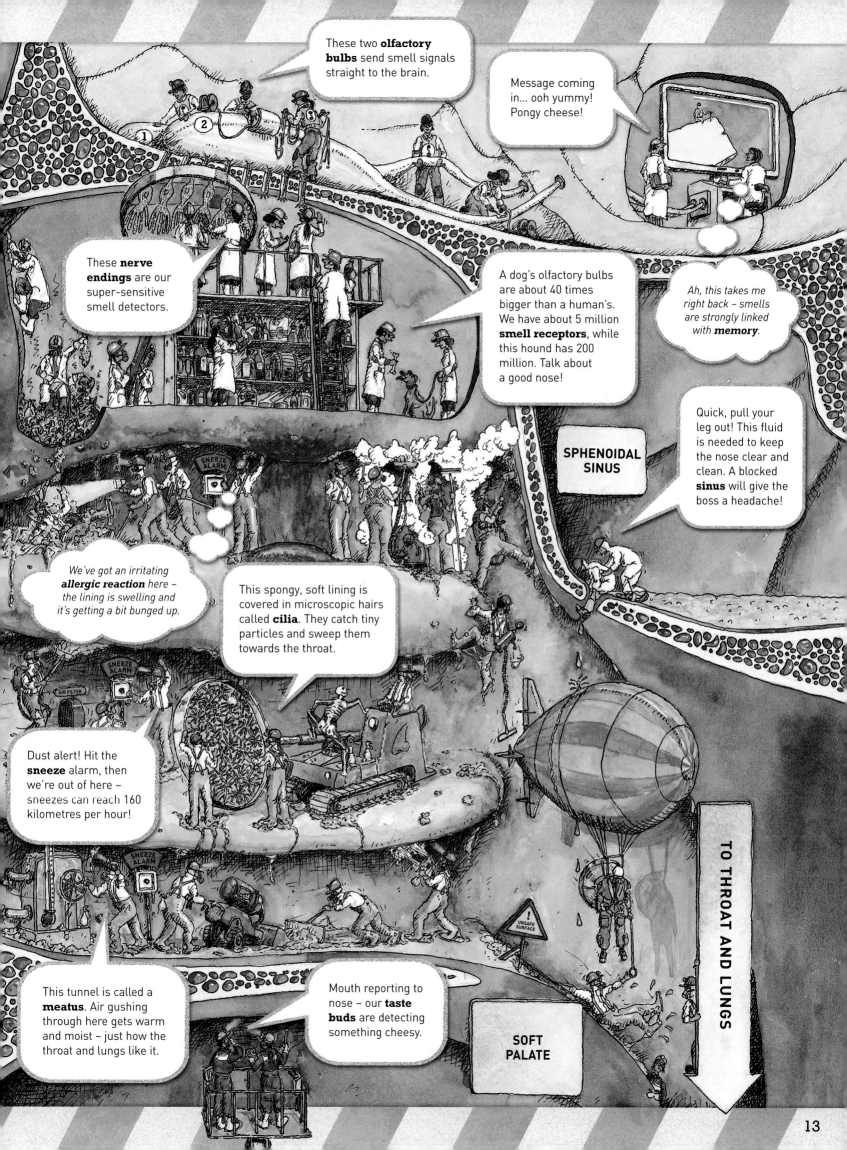

Mouth

Soaking in slurpy saliva, the mouth is a dangerous work zone. It mashes up almost anything in its path! It is the hatchway for food and drink and the exit-hole for coughs, hiccups and upchucks. This guzzling, grinding, churning, chomping machine is the first stage in your digestive system. Gulp!

YOU ARE HERE

Right team, time for a total tooth count... 8 biting **incisors**; 4 ripping **canines**; 20 grinding **molars** at the back. 32 in all – check!

This **uvula** helps us to make throaty sounds.

These **jaw-closing muscles** are the most powerful in the body. They chomp the teeth hard together like a monster grinding machine!

TONSIL DEPT

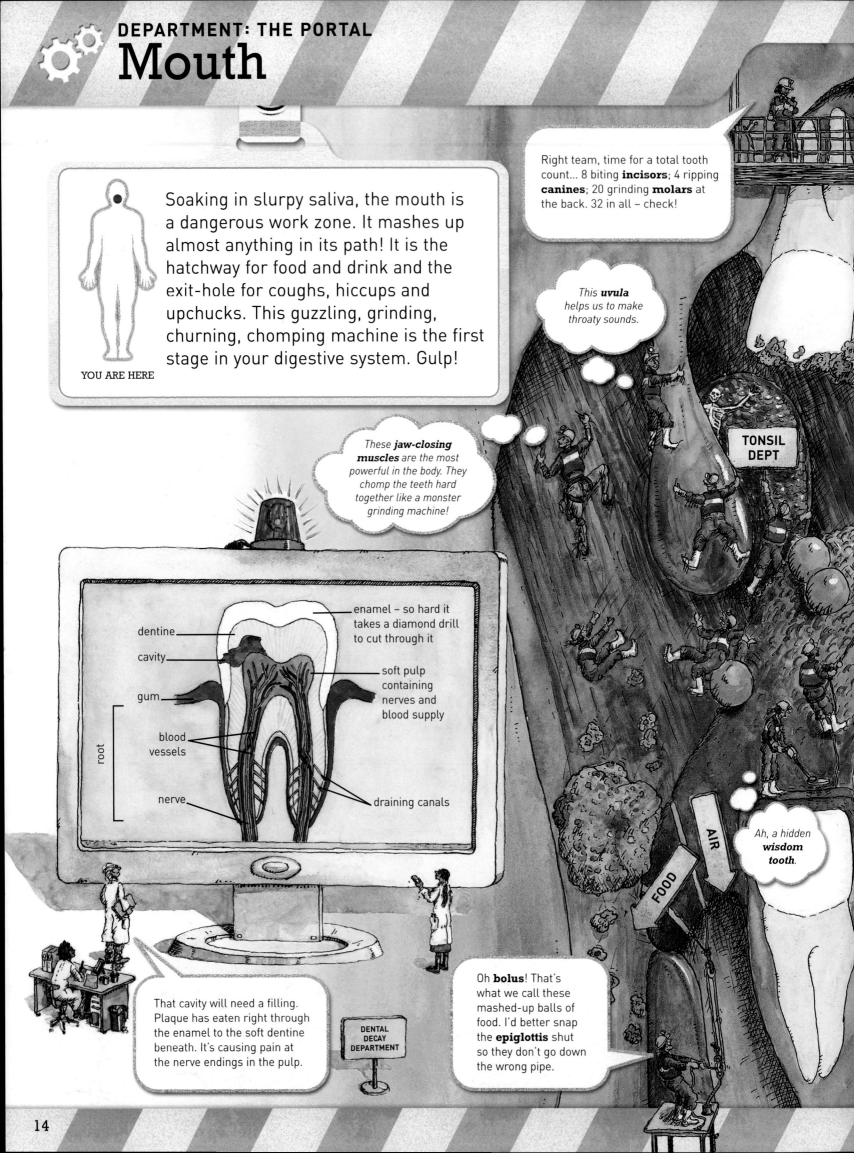

dentine

cavity

gum

root

blood vessels

nerve

enamel – so hard it takes a diamond drill to cut through it

soft pulp containing nerves and blood supply

draining canals

AIR

FOOD

Ah, a hidden **wisdom tooth**.

That cavity will need a filling. Plaque has eaten right through the enamel to the soft dentine beneath. It's causing pain at the nerve endings in the pulp.

DENTAL DECAY DEPARTMENT

Oh **bolus**! That's what we call these mashed-up balls of food. I'd better snap the **epiglottis** shut so they don't go down the wrong pipe.

Endocrine System

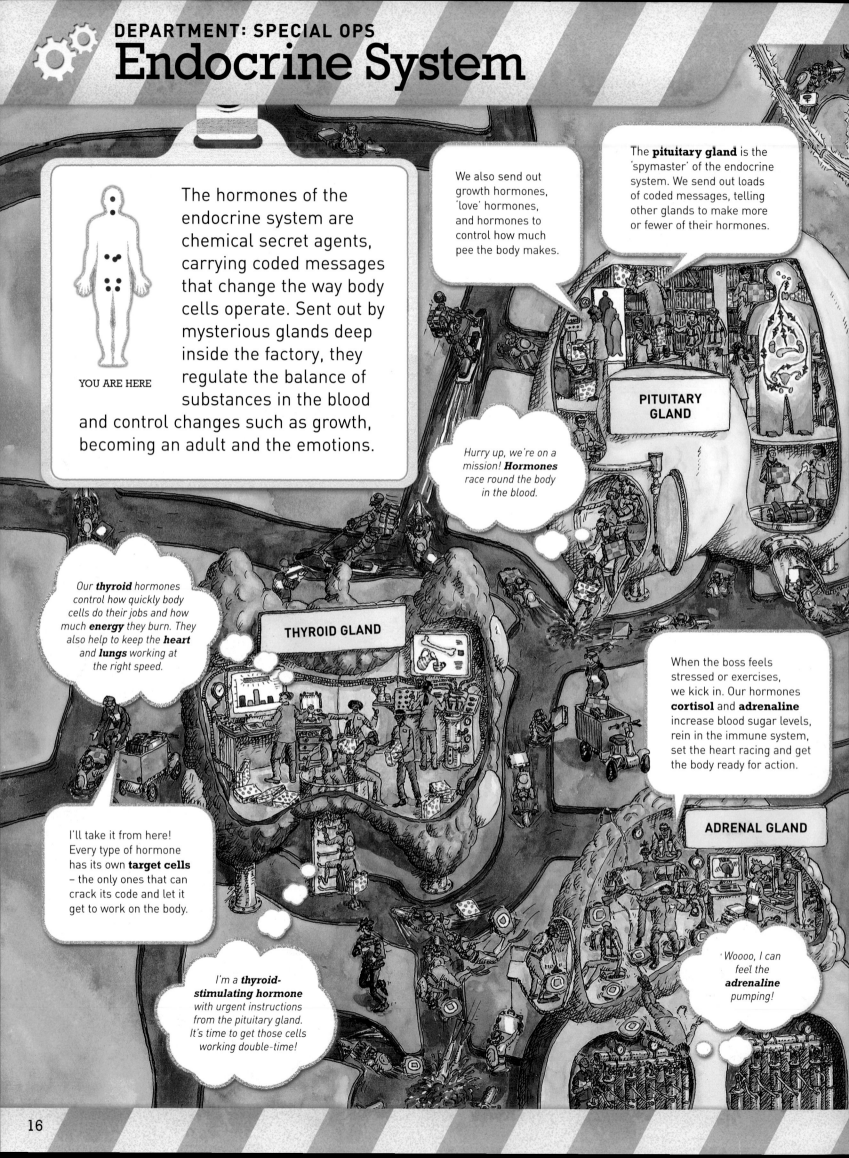

YOU ARE HERE

The hormones of the endocrine system are chemical secret agents, carrying coded messages that change the way body cells operate. Sent out by mysterious glands deep inside the factory, they regulate the balance of substances in the blood and control changes such as growth, becoming an adult and the emotions.

We also send out growth hormones, 'love' hormones, and hormones to control how much pee the body makes.

The **pituitary gland** is the 'spymaster' of the endocrine system. We send out loads of coded messages, telling other glands to make more or fewer of their hormones.

PITUITARY GLAND

Hurry up, we're on a mission! **Hormones** race round the body in the blood.

Our **thyroid** hormones control how quickly body cells do their jobs and how much **energy** they burn. They also help to keep the **heart** and **lungs** working at the right speed.

THYROID GLAND

When the boss feels stressed or exercises, we kick in. Our hormones **cortisol** and **adrenaline** increase blood sugar levels, rein in the immune system, set the heart racing and get the body ready for action.

ADRENAL GLAND

I'll take it from here! Every type of hormone has its own **target cells** – the only ones that can crack its code and let it get to work on the body.

I'm a **thyroid-stimulating hormone** with urgent instructions from the pituitary gland. It's time to get those cells working double-time!

Woooo, I can feel the **adrenaline** pumping!

Skin, Hair and Nails

Nails protect the ends of the fingers. They lie on a spongy nail bed and grow about 3 millimetres per month. They're made from the same material as hair.

Skin is the body's first line of defence. Its tough outer layer is made of old, **dead cells** – and we shed about 30,000 to 40,000 of them every day.

New skin cells form at the bottom of the **epidermis** and gradually move to the surface. My raking work is never done!

*Every person has a unique set of **fingerprints**. Only this Human Body Factory can make this exact mark!*

*Luckily for me, the **fingertips** are really **sensitive**. Special cells send messages to the brain, so you know how hard or gently to grip things.*

*The **dermis** is packed with **sensors** for touch, pain, heat and cold. Some react to pressure or ticklish vibrations, tee hee!*

YOU ARE HERE

The Human Body Factory is wrapped in a high-tech superskin that keeps it cool, watertight and protected from the world outside. The skin is the body's largest organ, covering about 2 square metres and weighing up to 4 kilograms. It's stuffed full of complex sensors and other gadgets, and can even mend itself when it picks up scuffs and tears.

One of the places we store fat at the factory is here, under the skin. **Subcutaneous fat** helps to keep the body warm, but it's best not to let this layer grow too large!

DERMIS

SUBCUTANEOUS FAT

DEPARTMENT: THE ENGINE ROOM
Heart

The beating hub of the Human Body Factory is the heart. This tireless, hard-working department pumps thousands of litres of blood around the body every day. It works with the lungs to make sure every body cell gets oxygen. It also helps the blood to deliver nutrients and dispose of waste.

YOU ARE HERE

The heart pumps blood in a constant cycle. First, the blood pours into two upper chambers called **atria**. When these are full, they contract, squirting blood down to the lower **ventricles**. Finally, the ventricles contract and squeeze blood out of the heart into the **arteries**.

atria
valves
ventricles

LUBB-DUBB! The **heartbeat** sound is created as blood passes from atria to ventricles and one set of **valves** closes (lubb). From the ventricles out of the heart a second set closes (dubb).

Make way in the **superior vena cava**! This blood has been round the body, delivering oxygen and collecting waste carbon dioxide. It needs pumping to the lungs.

TO THE BODY

In the **aorta** we transport oxygen-rich blood from the lungs towards the rest of the body.

TO THE LUNGS

FROM THE BODY

Phew, the **pressure** in here's enough to spurt blood across a room!

*Okay okay, I'm going as fast as I can through the **pulmonary artery**! Off to pick up more oxygen from the lungs...*

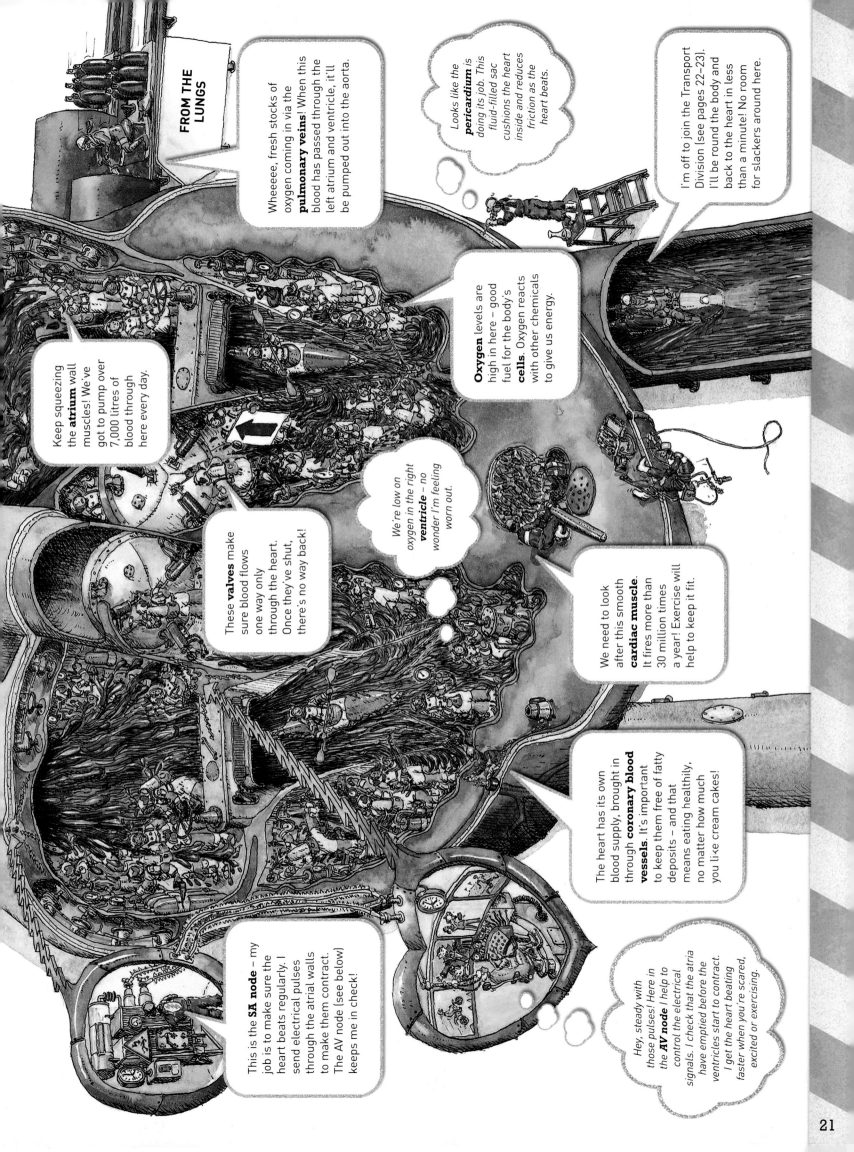

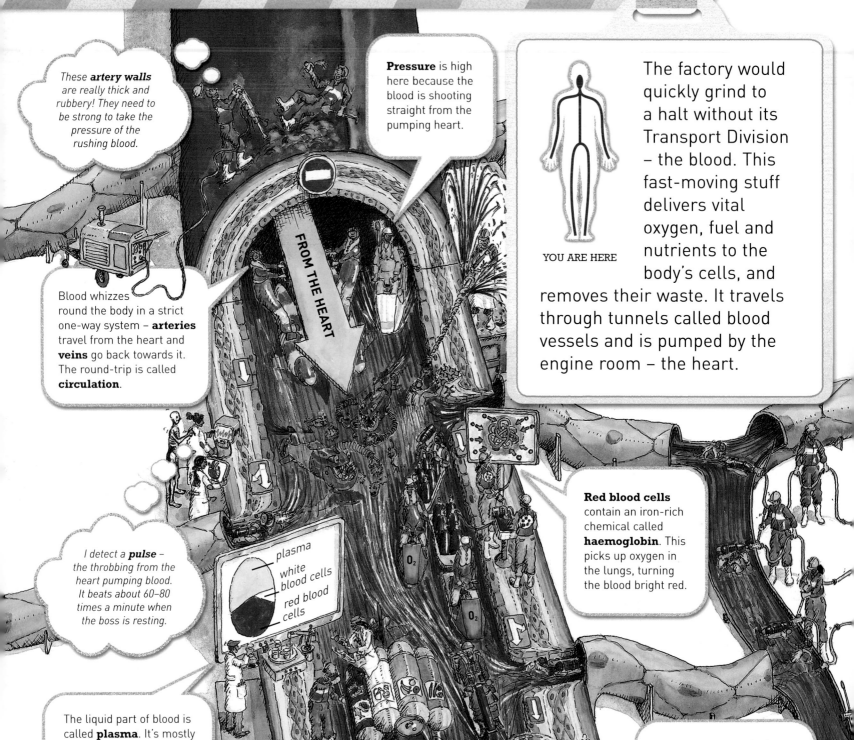

These **artery walls** are really thick and rubbery! They need to be strong to take the pressure of the rushing blood.

Pressure is high here because the blood is shooting straight from the pumping heart.

YOU ARE HERE

The factory would quickly grind to a halt without its Transport Division – the blood. This fast-moving stuff delivers vital oxygen, fuel and nutrients to the body's cells, and removes their waste. It travels through tunnels called blood vessels and is pumped by the engine room – the heart.

FROM THE HEART

Blood whizzes round the body in a strict one-way system – **arteries** travel from the heart and **veins** go back towards it. The round-trip is called **circulation**.

I detect a **pulse** – the throbbing from the heart pumping blood. It beats about 60–80 times a minute when the boss is resting.

plasma
white blood cells
red blood cells

Red blood cells contain an iron-rich chemical called **haemoglobin**. This picks up oxygen in the lungs, turning the blood bright red.

The liquid part of blood is called **plasma**. It's mostly salty water and is pale yellow in colour. Blood cells float in it, while other stuff is dissolved in it.

Blood pressure is the force with which the heart pumps blood through the blood vessels. It can rise during exercise, when your heart works harder.

The boss needs to cut down on fatty foods! They can cause excess **cholesterol**, which gunks up smaller arteries and blocks the blood supply to body cells.

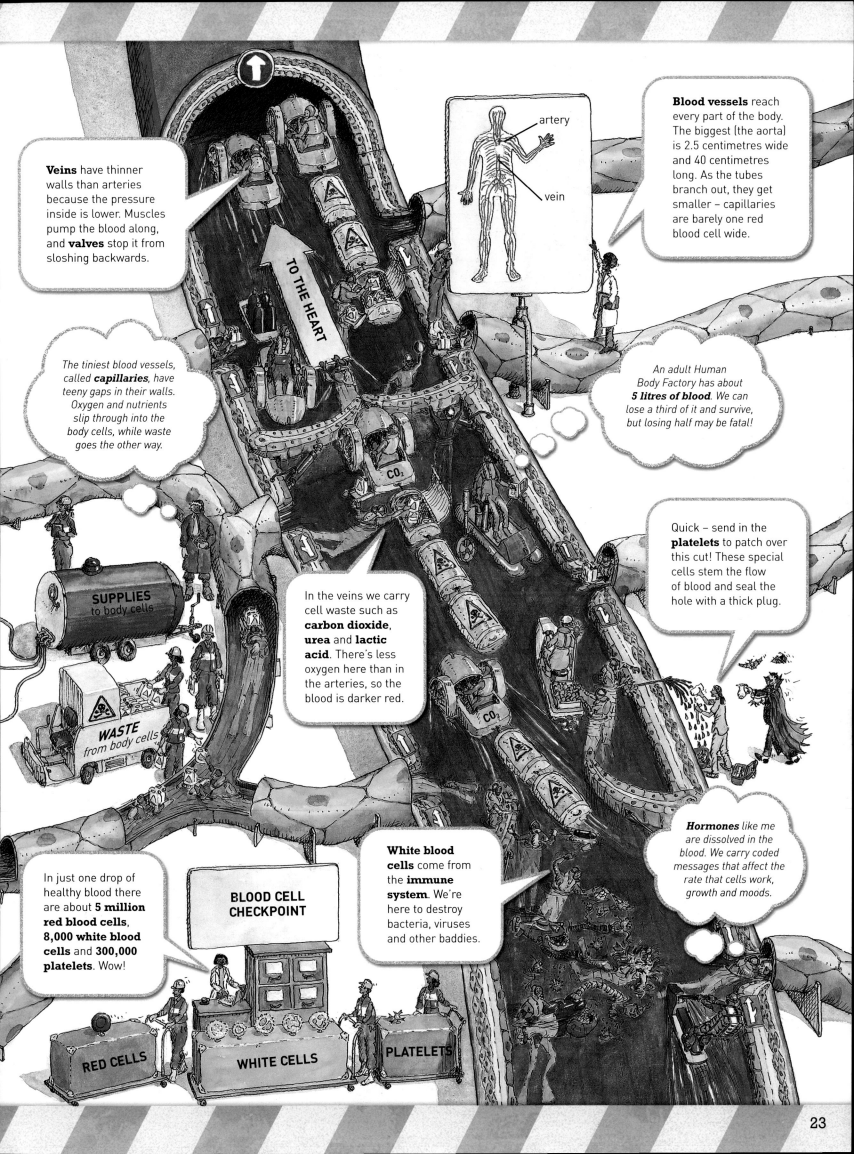

Veins have thinner walls than arteries because the pressure inside is lower. Muscles pump the blood along, and **valves** stop it from sloshing backwards.

TO THE HEART

artery

vein

Blood vessels reach every part of the body. The biggest (the aorta) is 2.5 centimetres wide and 40 centimetres long. As the tubes branch out, they get smaller – capillaries are barely one red blood cell wide.

The tiniest blood vessels, called **capillaries**, have teeny gaps in their walls. Oxygen and nutrients slip through into the body cells, while waste goes the other way.

An adult Human Body Factory has about **5 litres of blood**. We can lose a third of it and survive, but losing half may be fatal!

CO_2

CO_2

Quick – send in the **platelets** to patch over this cut! These special cells stem the flow of blood and seal the hole with a thick plug.

SUPPLIES to body cells

In the veins we carry cell waste such as **carbon dioxide**, **urea** and **lactic acid**. There's less oxygen here than in the arteries, so the blood is darker red.

WASTE from body cells

Hormones like me are dissolved in the blood. We carry coded messages that affect the rate that cells work, growth and moods.

In just one drop of healthy blood there are about **5 million red blood cells**, **8,000 white blood cells** and **300,000 platelets**. Wow!

BLOOD CELL CHECKPOINT

White blood cells come from the **immune system**. We're here to destroy bacteria, viruses and other baddies.

RED CELLS

WHITE CELLS

PLATELETS

Immune System

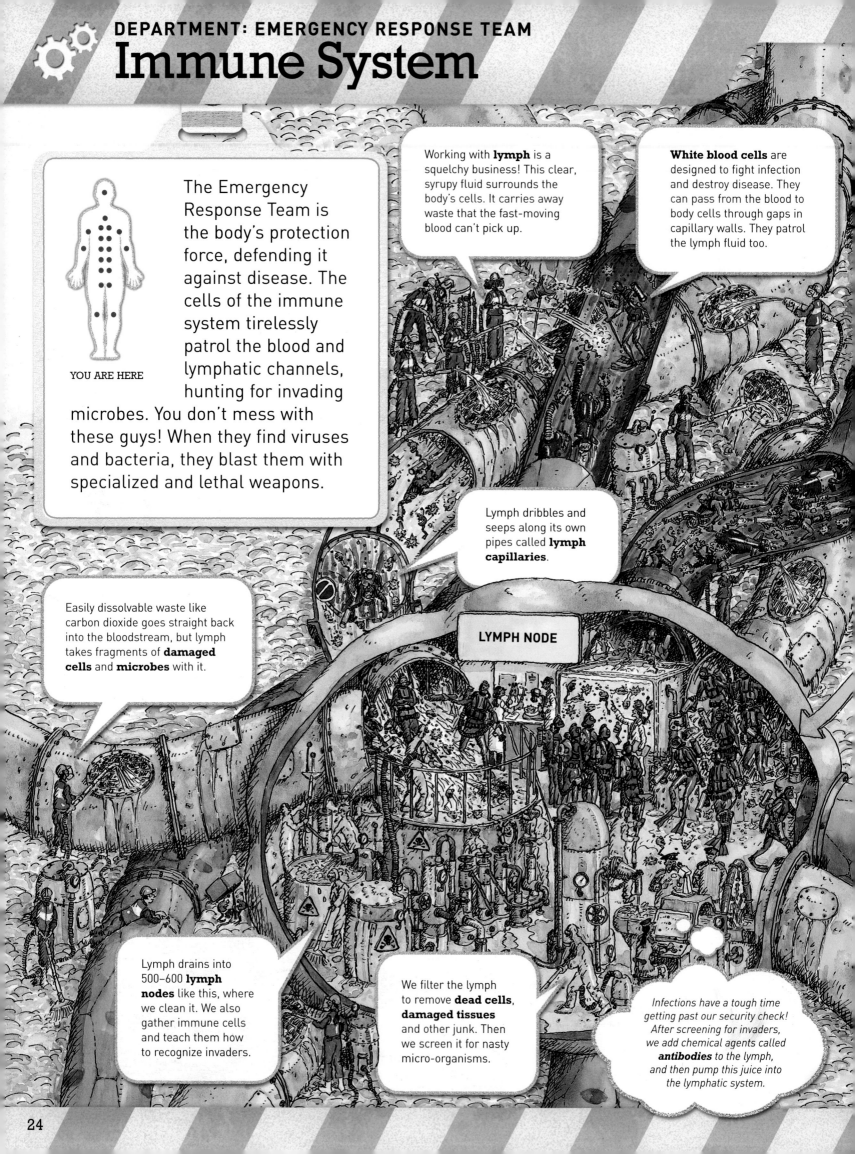

YOU ARE HERE

The Emergency Response Team is the body's protection force, defending it against disease. The cells of the immune system tirelessly patrol the blood and lymphatic channels, hunting for invading microbes. You don't mess with these guys! When they find viruses and bacteria, they blast them with specialized and lethal weapons.

Working with **lymph** is a squelchy business! This clear, syrupy fluid surrounds the body's cells. It carries away waste that the fast-moving blood can't pick up.

White blood cells are designed to fight infection and destroy disease. They can pass from the blood to body cells through gaps in capillary walls. They patrol the lymph fluid too.

Lymph dribbles and seeps along its own pipes called **lymph capillaries**.

Easily dissolvable waste like carbon dioxide goes straight back into the bloodstream, but lymph takes fragments of **damaged cells** and **microbes** with it.

LYMPH NODE

Lymph drains into 500–600 **lymph nodes** like this, where we clean it. We also gather immune cells and teach them how to recognize invaders.

We filter the lymph to remove **dead cells**, **damaged tissues** and other junk. Then we screen it for nasty micro-organisms.

Infections have a tough time getting past our security check! After screening for invaders, we add chemical agents called **antibodies** to the lymph, and then pump this juice into the lymphatic system.

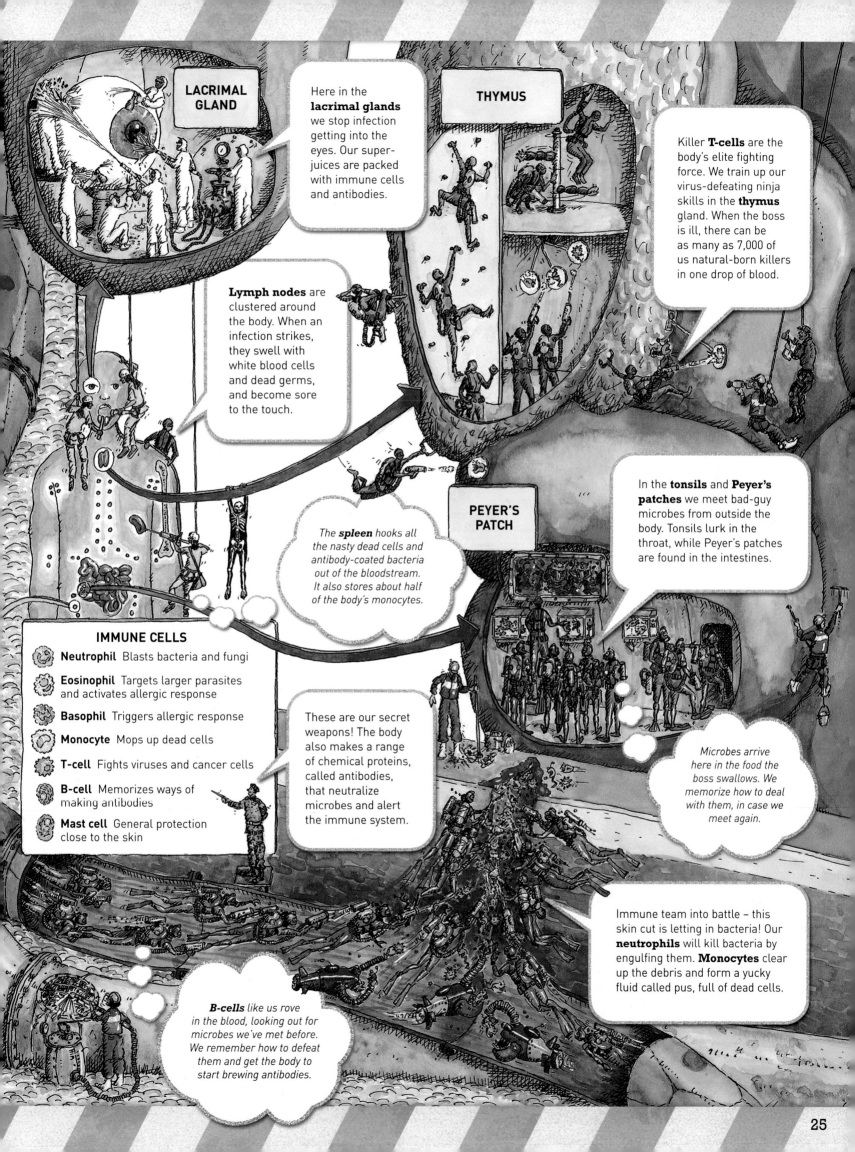

LACRIMAL GLAND

Here in the **lacrimal glands** we stop infection getting into the eyes. Our super-juices are packed with immune cells and antibodies.

THYMUS

Killer **T-cells** are the body's elite fighting force. We train up our virus-defeating ninja skills in the **thymus** gland. When the boss is ill, there can be as many as 7,000 of us natural-born killers in one drop of blood.

Lymph nodes are clustered around the body. When an infection strikes, they swell with white blood cells and dead germs, and become sore to the touch.

PEYER'S PATCH

In the **tonsils** and **Peyer's patches** we meet bad-guy microbes from outside the body. Tonsils lurk in the throat, while Peyer's patches are found in the intestines.

The **spleen** hooks all the nasty dead cells and antibody-coated bacteria out of the bloodstream. It also stores about half of the body's monocytes.

IMMUNE CELLS

Neutrophil Blasts bacteria and fungi

Eosinophil Targets larger parasites and activates allergic response

Basophil Triggers allergic response

Monocyte Mops up dead cells

T-cell Fights viruses and cancer cells

B-cell Memorizes ways of making antibodies

Mast cell General protection close to the skin

These are our secret weapons! The body also makes a range of chemical proteins, called antibodies, that neutralize microbes and alert the immune system.

Microbes arrive here in the food the boss swallows. We memorize how to deal with them, in case we meet again.

Immune team into battle – this skin cut is letting in bacteria! Our **neutrophils** will kill bacteria by engulfing them. **Monocytes** clear up the debris and form a yucky fluid called pus, full of dead cells.

B-cells like us rove in the blood, looking out for microbes we've met before. We remember how to defeat them and get the body to start brewing antibodies.

Bones and Joints

The Human Body Factory is built around a tough inner framework – the skeleton. This bundle of bones supports the body's weight, protects vital organs and provides anchor points for muscles to pull upon. Where bones meet at joints, a complex system of pulleys and cords allow the body to flex and bend. It's important to look after this department – after all, without it you'd be a floppy heap!

YOU ARE HERE

JOINT SHOP

Hinge	Pivot	Ball & socket	Gliding	Saddle
knee	neck	shoulder	backbone	thumb
elbow	forearm	hip	ankle, wrist	

This jelly-like stuff inside the bone is **bone marrow**. Its job is to make your blood cells – including 175 billion fresh red blood cells every day. Surrounding the marrow is a soft but strong honeycomb of **spongy bone**.

Wow, 206 bones in an adult **skeleton!**

The hard outer layer is called **compact bone**. It's packed with living **osteocyte** cells that have their own blood supply. Bones may seem like dead things, but in fact they're very much alive!

Get your **joints** here! Wherever two bones meet, you need the right joint to let them move properly. There are also some fixed joints, like the ones in your skull.

The knee is the body's largest joint – and one of the most hard-working. Between the bones is a pocket of **synovial fluid**, which oils the joint to keep it moving smoothly.

Bone food on its way! **Calcium** helps to keep bones hard and strong – we get it from dairy products and even some vegetables, fruits and nuts. Vitamin D from sunlight is good for bones too.

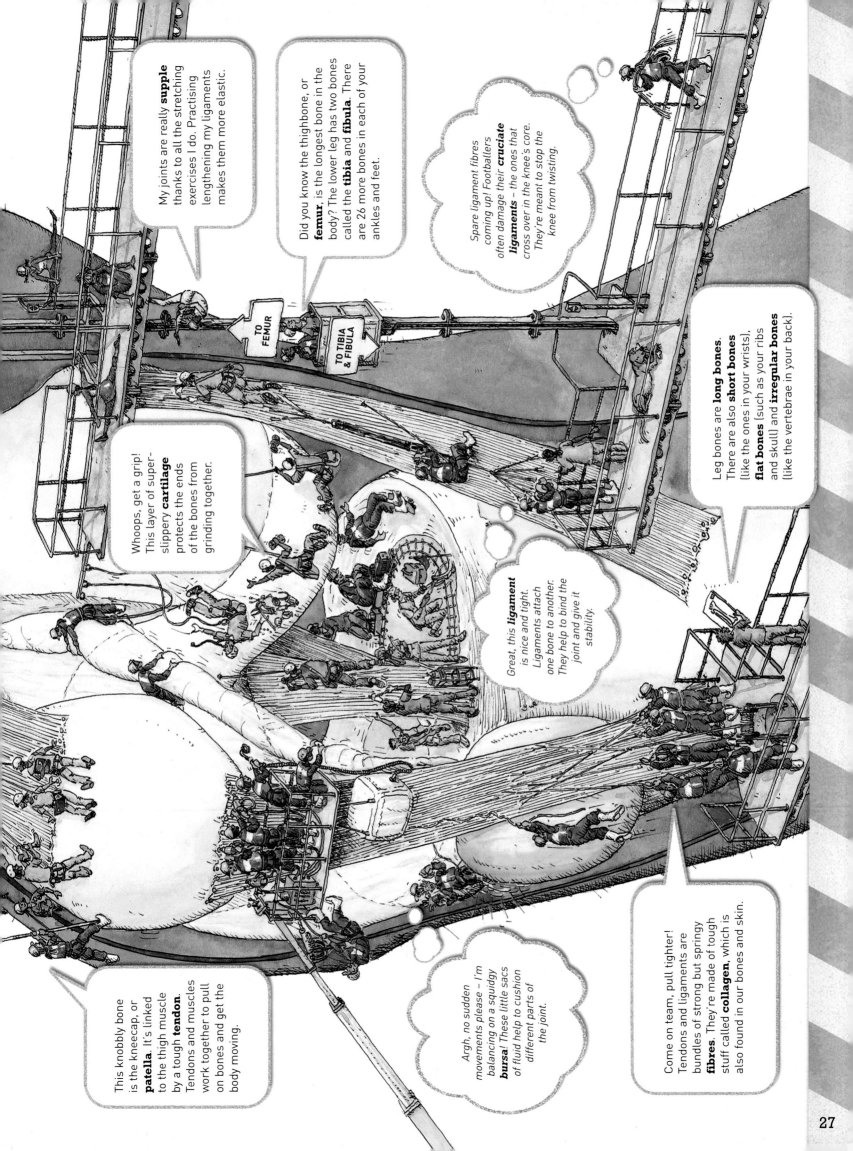

Muscles

Muscles work in pairs to pull on bones. To lift the lower arm, the **biceps** here **contracts**, or tightens up.

Come on blood team, keep the **oxygen**, **water** and **glucose** coming! The muscles need these to make and burn their fuel, called **ATP**. Without it, the boss would get weak!

While the biceps contracts, the **triceps** underneath the arm **relaxes** and lengthens out.

Muscles are made up of lots of stringy **fibres**. Only one-third of all fibres contract at the same time when the muscle is working at full power.

All this muscle action **burns energy** and warms the body. I'm taking a break, but not for long! To lower the arm, it's the triceps that do the work.

Uh-oh – I'm reading a build-up of **lactic acid** waste. If we don't get oxygen into the muscle fast, I'm afraid the boss will get **cramp**.

Electrical impulses from tiny **nerve fibres** trigger each strand of muscle to contract. Skeletal muscles like the biceps are controlled by the boss's brain.

Your body has about **320 muscle pairs** and they make up over half of your weight. Training them up can make you strong like me!

Show-off! Bet you don't know that **blood flow** to the muscles increases by up to 12 times during exercise.

BLOOD SUPPLIES

WATER

GLUCOSE

LACTIC ACID DISPOSAL

RELAX

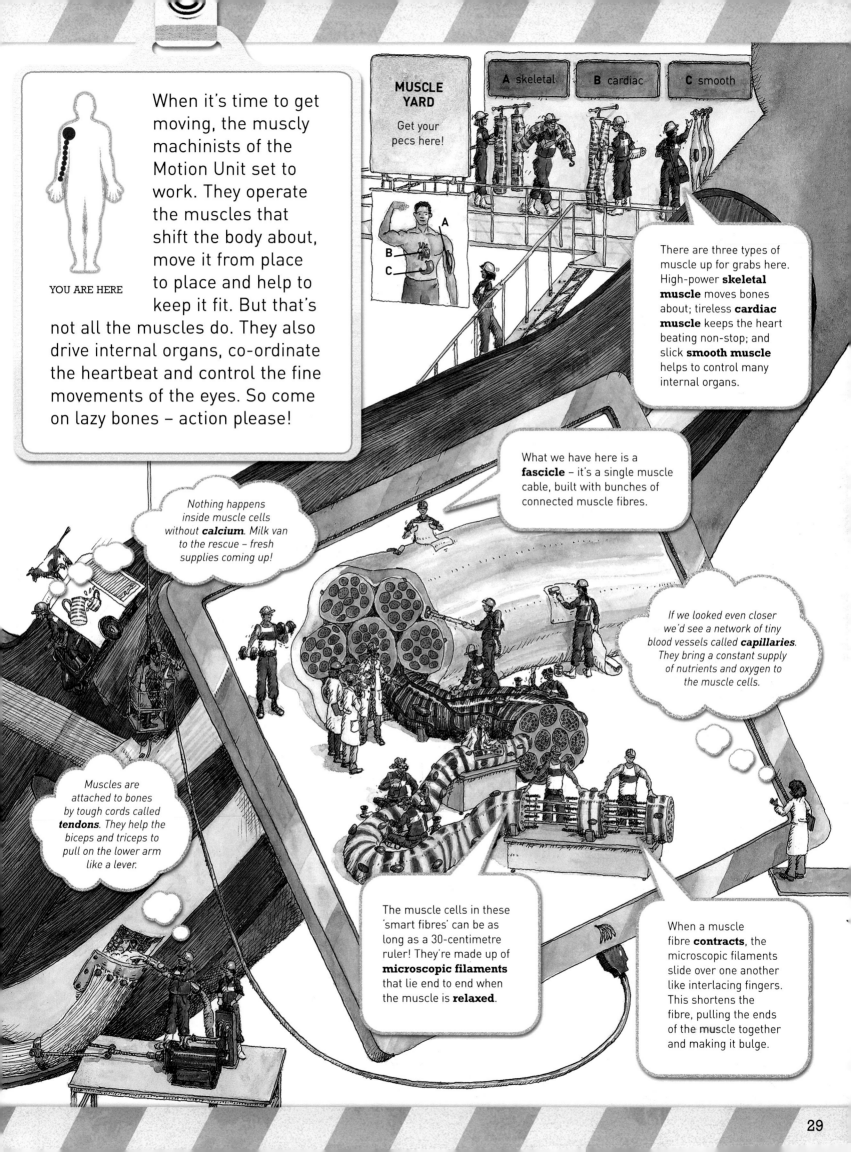

Watch how this **reflex** bypasses the brain! The signal zaps in a short-cut, down a sensory nerve to the spinal cord then back along a motor nerve. This jerks a limb quickly out of harm's way.

*Neurons fire signals from one to another across a **synapse**, which looks like this.*

Electricity is building up – it won't be long until the neuron fires!

*All 33 **vertebrae** are in good order. These backbones form a strong, bendy column to protect the spinal cord.*

NEURON TEST CENTRE

dendrite

axon

cell body

VOLTS

Ouch! **Pain** hurts, but it's there to warn the body that it's in danger. The spinal cord can let pain through or partly block it, depending on the level set by the brain.

These wiry bits carry the neuron's electrical signals. **Dendrites** receive signals from other neurons. **Axons** pass them on.

ON OFF

PAIN GAUGE

ON OFF

Nerve signals zap up and down at 290 kilometres per hour. How's that for instant messaging!

The spinal cord and brain make up the **central nervous system**. From here, nerves branch out to every part of the body. That's the **peripheral nervous system**.

Sensory and motor nerves are grouped into bundles called **fascicles**. There are blood vessels in here too. If they get squished, you might find yourself with pins and needles!

YOU ARE HERE

The Human Body Factory tingles and twitches with electricity, and the Info and Comms Division are the sparky workforce who wire up the body to the brain. They zap electrical signals along networks of branching nerve wires. This allows the brain to control muscles, operate internal organs and monitor what's going on inside and outside the factory.

Lungs

YOU ARE HERE

The lungs are where Human Body Factory workers go to keep fit. Their job is to get vital oxygen into the body and force poisonous carbon dioxide out. Air enters and leaves the lungs through a maze of branching tubes, which end in tiny gas exchange pods. You need a lot of puff to work in this department. Take a deep breath!

We're here to keep the **intercostal muscles** working. They have to lift and lower the **ribcage** every time we breathe – that's around 20,000 times a day!

OK team, check the **cartilage** rings that keep these big air pipes open. There are 2,400 kilometres of tubes in here. The tiniest ones are called **bronchioles**.

When you **breathe in**, your diaphragm (beneath the lungs) pulls downwards. At the same time, intercostal muscles (in your chest) lift your ribs up and outwards. This creates space for air to rush into your lungs. They inflate just like balloons!

You **breathe out** when your diaphragm and intercostal muscles relax. The diaphragm springs upwards, the ribs close in, and air whistles out of your lungs to leave through your nose or mouth.

Good, a thin layer of fluid lining the **pleura**. This covering cushions and protects the lungs as you breathe.

Keep pulling down on the **diaphragm**! This sheet of muscle is like a set of industrial bellows, forcing air in and out of the lungs.

Liver and Gall Bladder

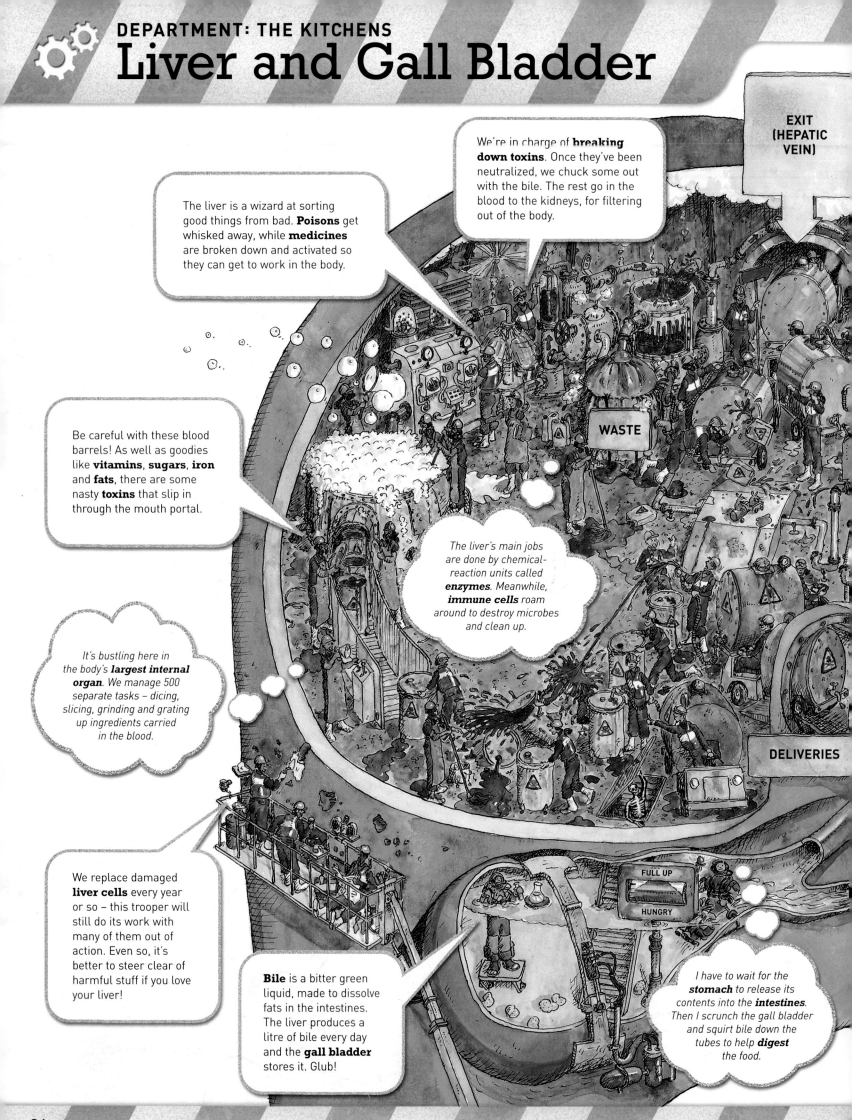

EXIT
(HEPATIC
VEIN)

We're in charge of **breaking down toxins**. Once they've been neutralized, we chuck some out with the bile. The rest go in the blood to the kidneys, for filtering out of the body.

The liver is a wizard at sorting good things from bad. **Poisons** get whisked away, while **medicines** are broken down and activated so they can get to work in the body.

Be careful with these blood barrels! As well as goodies like **vitamins**, **sugars**, **iron** and **fats**, there are some nasty **toxins** that slip in through the mouth portal.

WASTE

The liver's main jobs are done by chemical-reaction units called **enzymes**. Meanwhile, **immune cells** roam around to destroy microbes and clean up.

It's bustling here in the body's **largest internal organ**. We manage 500 separate tasks – dicing, slicing, grinding and grating up ingredients carried in the blood.

DELIVERIES

We replace damaged **liver cells** every year or so – this trooper will still do its work with many of them out of action. Even so, it's better to steer clear of harmful stuff if you love your liver!

FULL UP

HUNGRY

Bile is a bitter green liquid, made to dissolve fats in the intestines. The liver produces a litre of bile every day and the **gall bladder** stores it. Glub!

I have to wait for the **stomach** to release its contents into the **intestines**. Then I scrunch the gall bladder and squirt bile down the tubes to help **digest** the food.

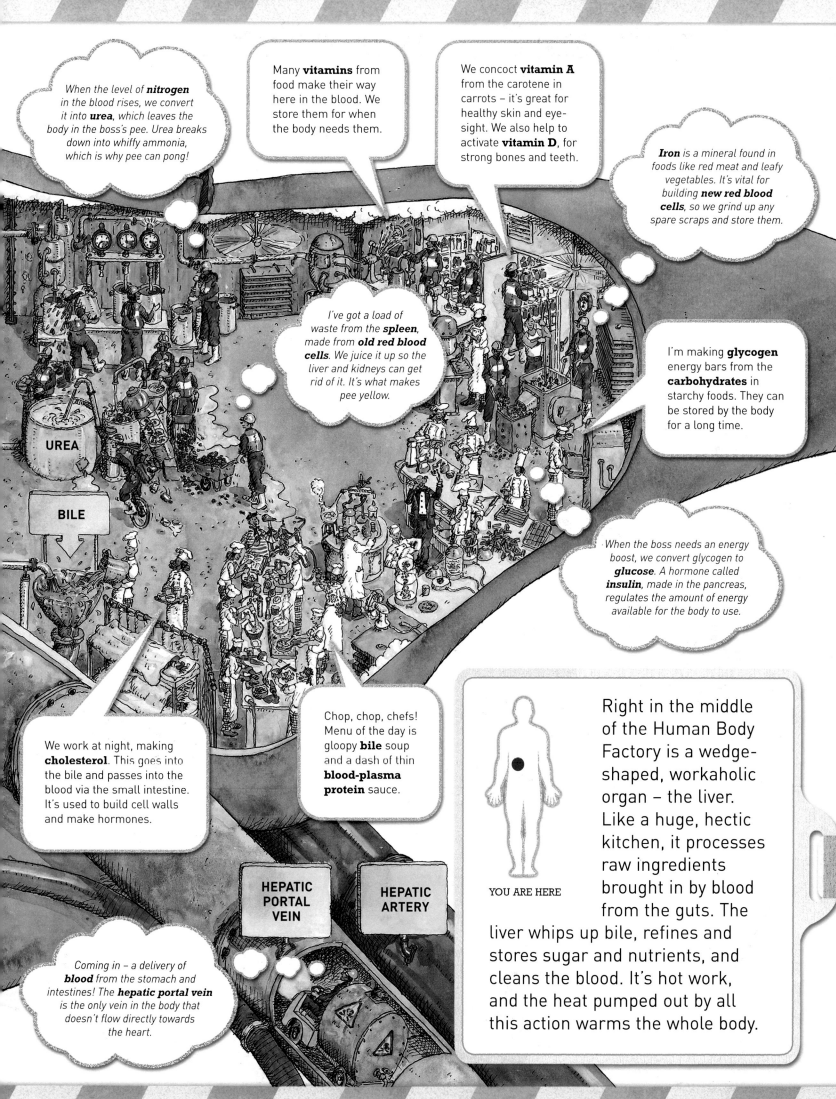

Kidneys and Bladder

The kidneys are a pair of steamy, gushy treatment plants, where toxic waste and excess water are removed from the blood. These complex, high-pressure filtering units clean 1,750 litres of blood every day. They also produce about 1.5 litres of urine, which flows to a bag called the bladder before exiting the body for good.

YOU ARE HERE

*Wow, there are 65 kilometres of nephrons in the kidney. No wonder the blood comes out clean! I'm taking it back down the **renal vein** to the rest of the body.*

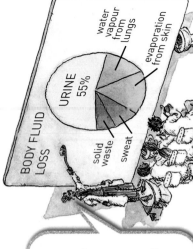

BODY FLUID LOSS

URINE 55%

water vapour from lungs

evaporation from skin

solid waste

sweat

The body is about two-thirds water, but we need to keep the balance right. We get rid of excess water in various ways. As you can see, the main one is **urination** (peeing).

Shipment of dirty blood coming in! Blood in the **renal artery** contains waste from the body and needs to be cleaned.

DIRTY BLOOD

CLEAN BLOOD

TO BLADDER

ADRENAL GLAND

Phew, I'm tired. Here in the **kidneys**, we filter the body's blood at least 300 times a day. We also help to balance the volume of fluids and salts in the body.

In this section we remove any useful **sugars**, **salts**, **minerals** and **proteins** from the urine and put them back into the blood.

*The watery parts of the blood, along with waste chemicals and some important nutrients, get squeezed out under **high pressure**. They are turned into a clear yellow liquid called **urine**.*

Each filtering unit is called a **nephron**. There are around a million of them in each kidney – and they're tiny. Here's a close-up look at one.

The high-pressure filter works a bit like a coffee machine. Psssssst.

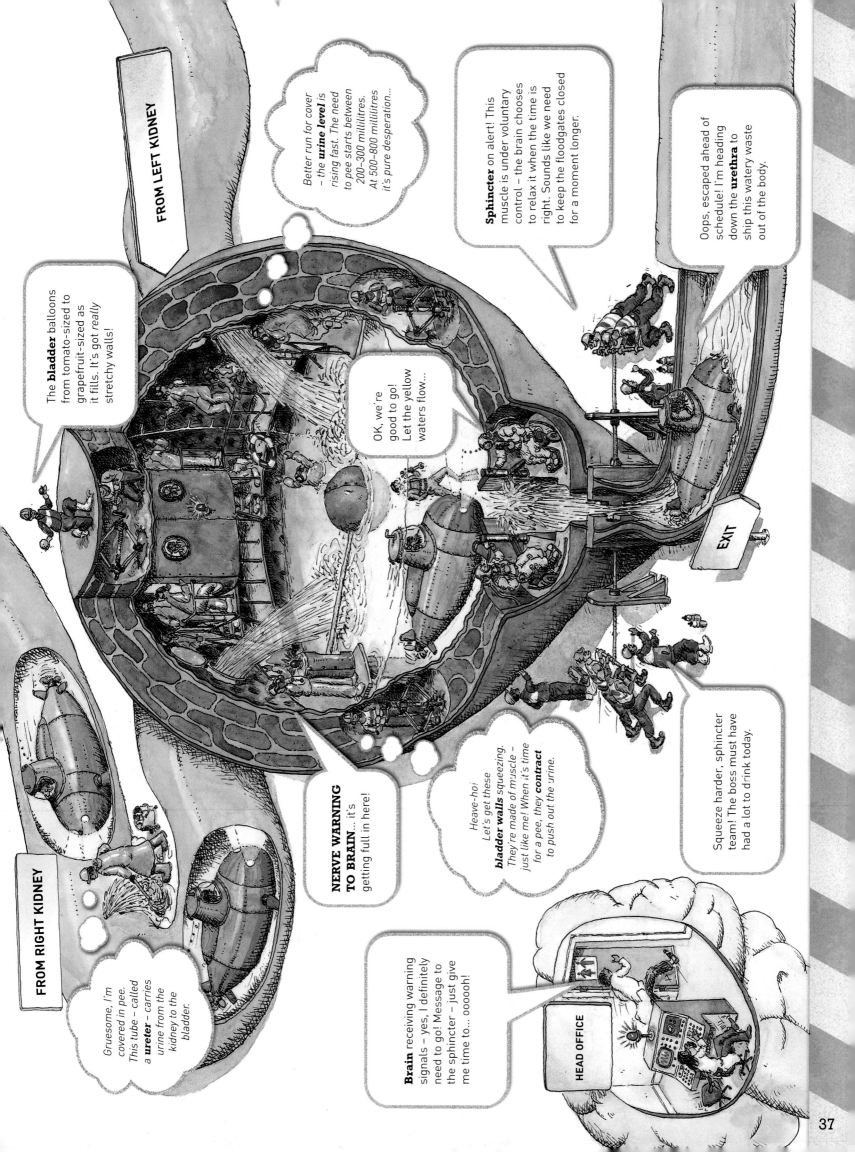

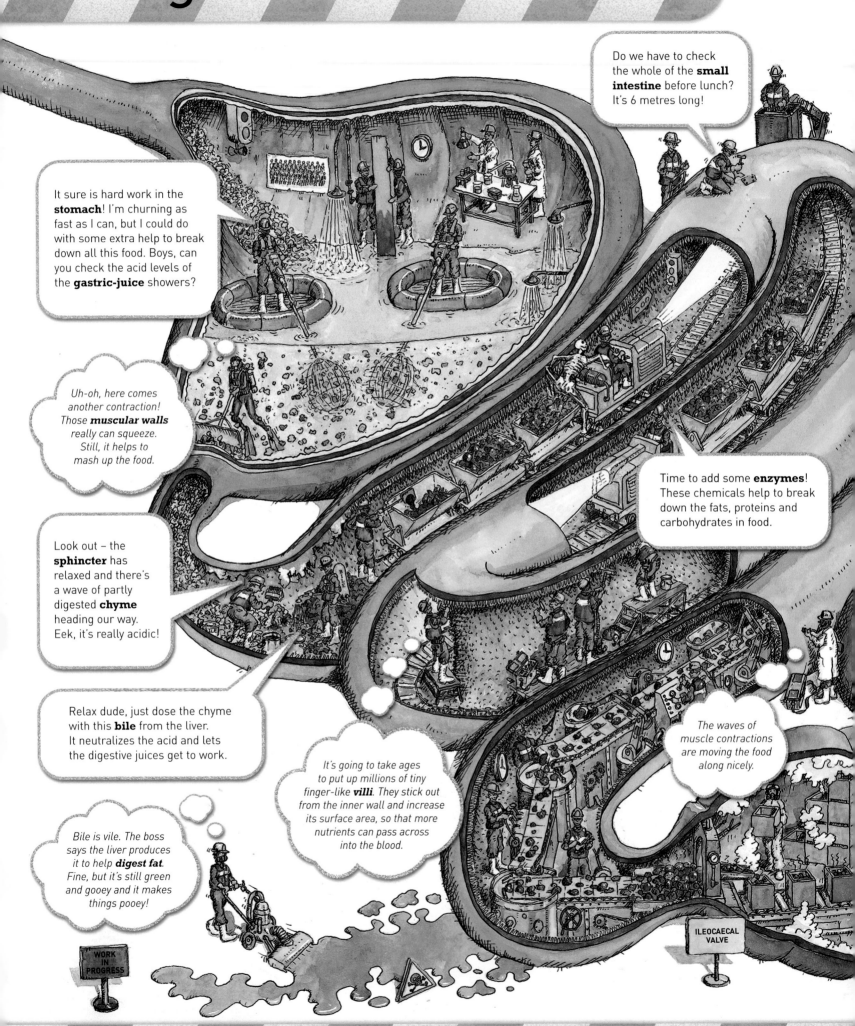

Do we have to check the whole of the **small intestine** before lunch? It's 6 metres long!

It sure is hard work in the **stomach**! I'm churning as fast as I can, but I could do with some extra help to break down all this food. Boys, can you check the acid levels of the **gastric-juice** showers?

Uh-oh, here comes another contraction! **Those muscular walls** *really can squeeze. Still, it helps to mash up the food.*

Time to add some **enzymes**! These chemicals help to break down the fats, proteins and carbohydrates in food.

Look out – the **sphincter** has relaxed and there's a wave of partly digested **chyme** heading our way. Eek, it's really acidic!

Relax dude, just dose the chyme with this **bile** from the liver. It neutralizes the acid and lets the digestive juices get to work.

It's going to take ages to put up millions of tiny finger-like **villi**. *They stick out from the inner wall and increase its surface area, so that more nutrients can pass across into the blood.*

The waves of muscle contractions are moving the food along nicely.

Bile is vile. The boss says the liver produces it to help **digest fat**. *Fine, but it's still green and gooey and it makes things pooey!*

WORK IN PROGRESS

ILEOCAECAL VALVE

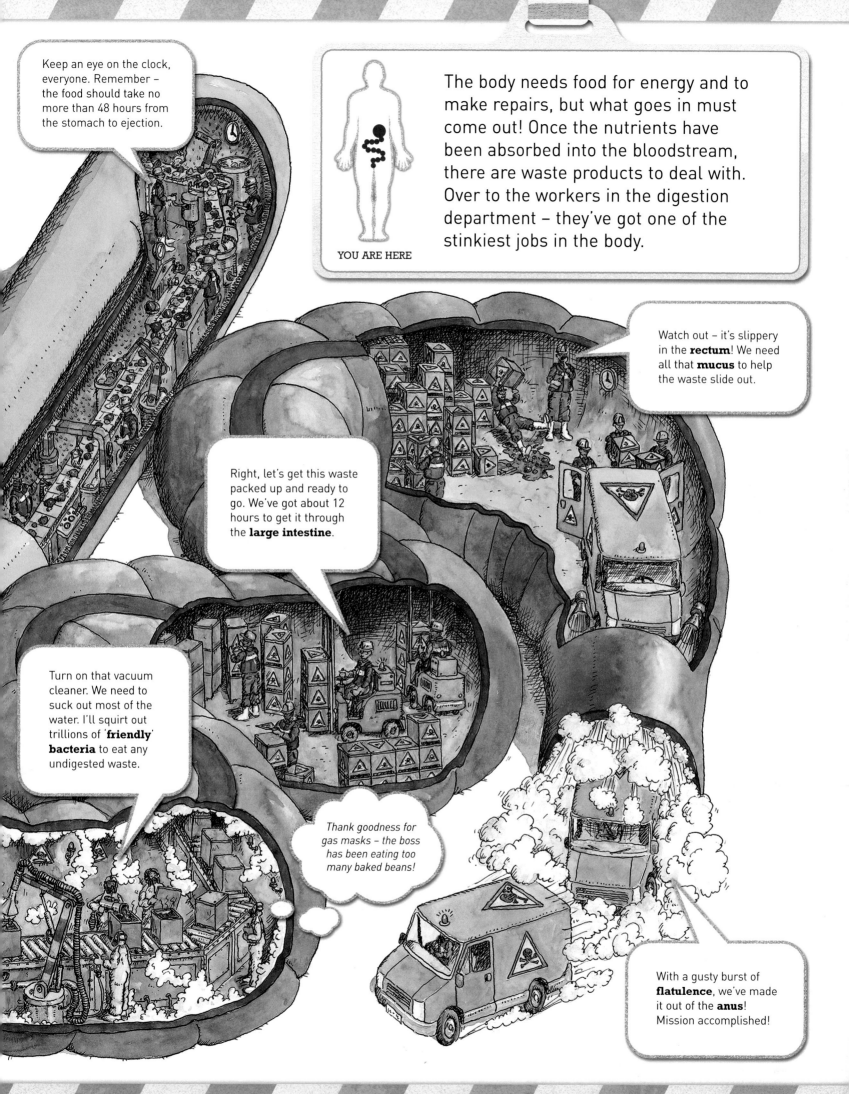

Reproduction

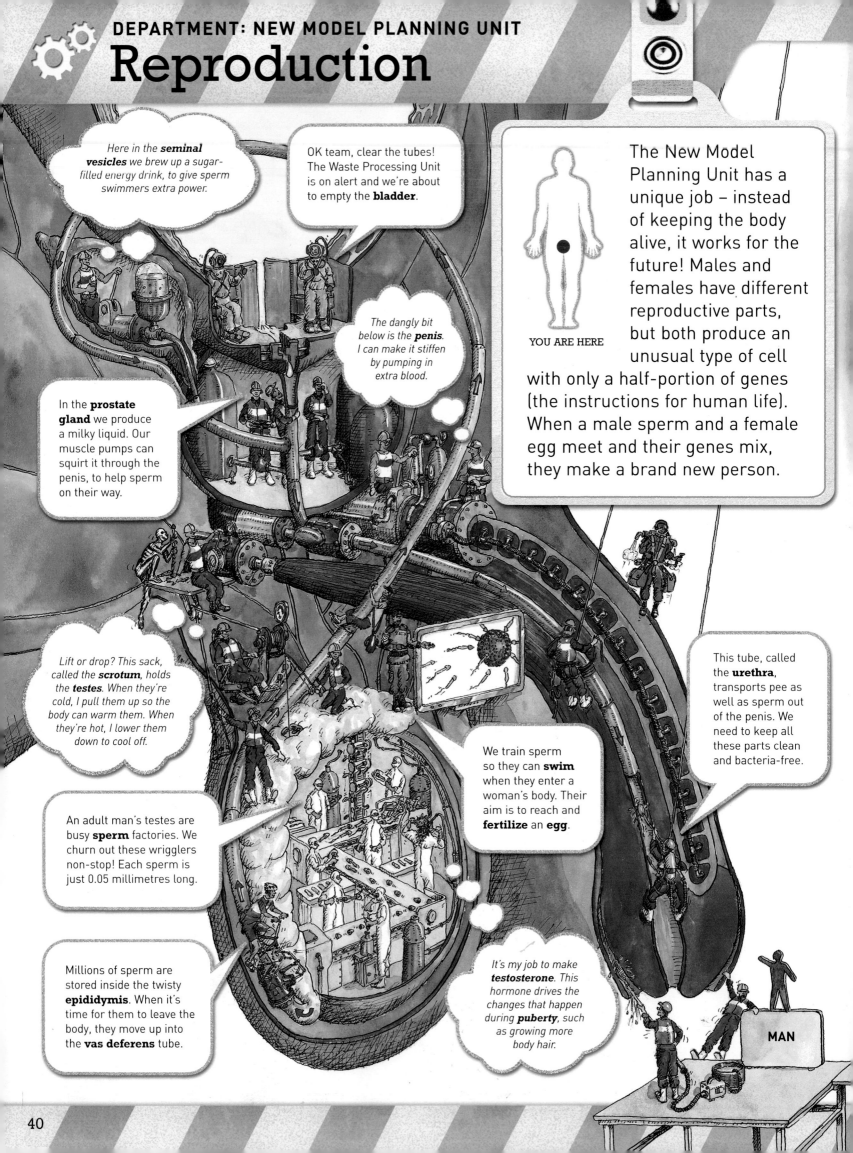

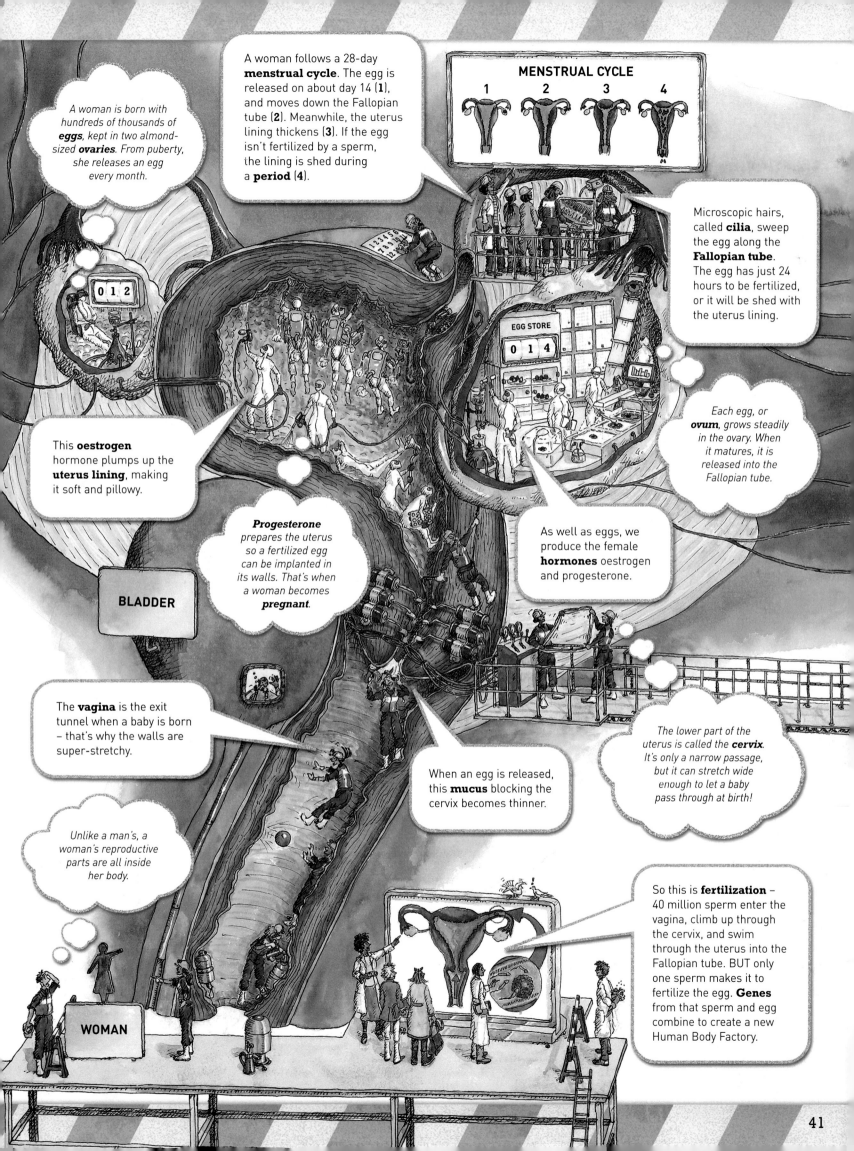

Pregnancy

UTERUS

Woo hoo! We've got a **fertilization**! Millions of sperm may reach the egg, but only one winner gets through its outer wall.

*We need more **progesterone** to plump up this lining.*

FROM OVARY

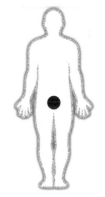

DAY 1

DAY 3

DAY 4

The sperm and egg fuse to form a single **cell**. In 24 hours this divides in two. It keeps dividing, and after about three days it's a ball of lots of cells.

Making a teeny-weeny new model is one of the most incredible things a Human Body Factory can do. The female body contains all the equipment needed to grow a new unit, but first one of her eggs must join with a male's sperm. It takes about 40 weeks of pregnancy to develop the new model to the stage where it can survive in the outside world.

YOU ARE HERE

Ready for **implantation**! The ball of cells now settles into the **uterus wall**. Parts of it develop separately to form the yolk sac, placenta and amniotic sac.

*We don't need this **yolk sac** now the baby is getting food from its mum.*

Good, the **amniotic sac** is strong! This fluid-filled bag protects the baby from bumps.

The **placenta** lets oxygen and nutrients pass from the mum's blood to the baby's. Waste goes in the other direction – but the two blood supplies never mix. The **umbilical cord** links the baby to the placenta.

placenta

umbilical cord

mother's blood – nutrients

baby's blood

waste

*There's not much thinking going on yet, but the **brain** is definitely starting to take shape!*

At this stage, the developing baby is called an **embryo**. It's only the size of a pea.

6 WEEKS

Excellent, the **heart** is just coming online – we have a pulse!

*It doesn't look very human yet – the limbs are just buds, the **hands** and **feet** are webbed and it's got a **tail**!*

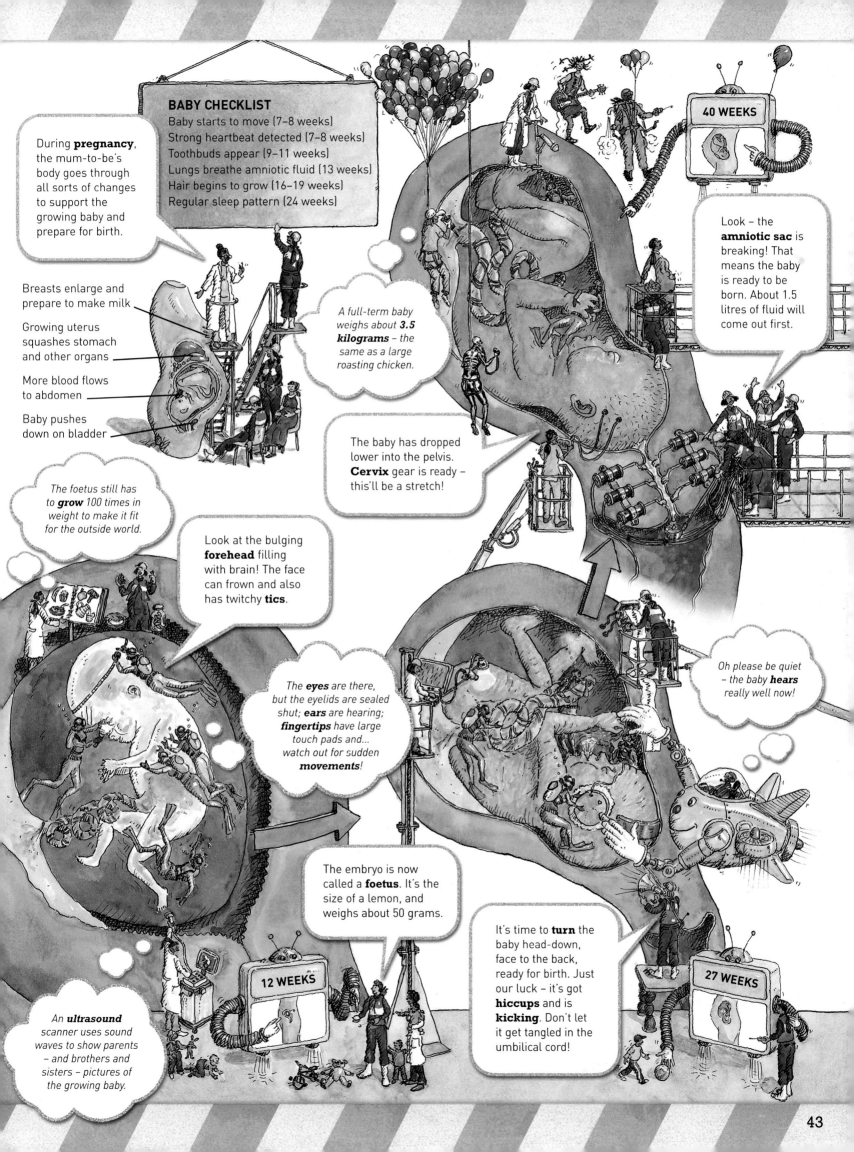

BABY CHECKLIST
Baby starts to move (7–8 weeks)
Strong heartbeat detected (7–8 weeks)
Toothbuds appear (9–11 weeks)
Lungs breathe amniotic fluid (13 weeks)
Hair begins to grow (16–19 weeks)
Regular sleep pattern (24 weeks)

During **pregnancy**, the mum-to-be's body goes through all sorts of changes to support the growing baby and prepare for birth.

Breasts enlarge and prepare to make milk

Growing uterus squashes stomach and other organs

More blood flows to abdomen

Baby pushes down on bladder

A full-term baby weighs about **3.5 kilograms** – the same as a large roasting chicken.

The foetus still has to **grow** 100 times in weight to make it fit for the outside world.

Look at the bulging **forehead** filling with brain! The face can frown and also has twitchy **tics**.

The baby has dropped lower into the pelvis. **Cervix** gear is ready – this'll be a stretch!

40 WEEKS

Look – the **amniotic sac** is breaking! That means the baby is ready to be born. About 1.5 litres of fluid will come out first.

The **eyes** are there, but the eyelids are sealed shut; **ears** are hearing; **fingertips** have large touch pads and... watch out for sudden **movements**!

Oh please be quiet – the baby **hears** really well now!

The embryo is now called a **foetus**. It's the size of a lemon, and weighs about 50 grams.

12 WEEKS

It's time to **turn** the baby head-down, face to the back, ready for birth. Just our luck – it's got **hiccups** and is **kicking**. Don't let it get tangled in the umbilical cord!

27 WEEKS

An **ultrasound** scanner uses sound waves to show parents – and brothers and sisters – pictures of the growing baby.

Amazing Body Facts

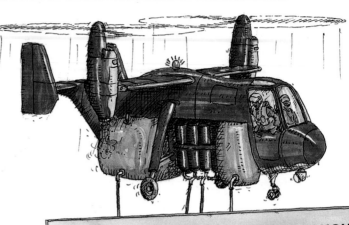

From the moment you leave your mother's womb, pop out into the world and take your first breath, your body is working hard to keep you up and running. It does a million marvellous things for you – like reading this book, for instance! Life is full of brain-boggling surprises...

THE HUMAN BODY CONTAINS ENOUGH:

Carbon to make about 900 pencils
Nitrogen to fill a fizzy drinks can
Phosphorus to make 2,000 matches
Iron for a standard nail
Sulphur to de-flea a dog
Fat to make 7 bars of soap
Water to fill a beer barrel!

HUMAN BODY FACT FILE

Number of bones: 206*

Average body temperature: 37°C

Average pulse rate: 60–90 beats per minute; athletes as low as 40 bpm*

Number of muscles: approx 650

Average brain weight: 1.4 kilograms*

Number of brain cells: more than 10 billion

Number of brain cells lost every day: 85,000

Total dead skin shed in a lifetime: approx 18 kilograms

Number of cell types: approx 220

Average total blood volume: 5 litres*

Total surface area of skin: approx 1.86 m²*

Total surface area of alveoli (in lungs): approx 70 m²*

* These facts refer to an adult Human Body Factory only (the others refer to all body factories)

The ridges on your fingers can feel minuscule bumps 0.001 millimetres across – about a hundred times smaller than anything you can see with your eyes!

Glossary

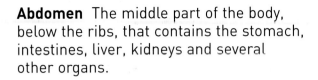

Abdomen The middle part of the body, below the ribs, that contains the stomach, intestines, liver, kidneys and several other organs.

Adrenal gland An organ that sits on top of each kidney and responds to stress by making hormones such as adrenaline and cortisol.

Antibodies Proteins made by white blood cells as part of the body's immune system, to attack germs and help fight infection.

Bacteria Microscopic single-celled organisms, also called microbes or germs; some cause infection in the body while others are 'friendly' bacteria that live in the intestines and on the skin.

Blind spot The point at the back of the eye where nerves lining the retina collect and turn towards the brain; there are no light-sensitive cells at the blind spot, so it is unable to see.

Brainstem The lower part of the brain, found at the top of the spinal cord, which controls breathing, heart rate and many other basic processes needed for survival.

Carbohydrate A component of food that the body converts to sugar (glucose) for energy.

Cardiovascular system The system that transports blood around the body, powered by the heart.

Cartilage Tough but flexible material that protects the ends of bones at joints; it also gives structure to body parts such as the nose, outer ear and tubes in the lungs and throat.

Cell The body's building block; cells make all the body's tissues and organs, and do all its basic jobs.

Cerebral cortex The highly folded, 'wrinkly' outer part of the cerebrum (brain); made of grey matter, which carries out much of the information processing in the brain.

Cholesterol A chemical, made in the liver from fats in the food we eat, which is used to build cell walls; too much cholesterol in the blood can damage blood vessels and lead to heart problems.

Chyme A gloopy, creamy fluid that leaves the stomach and passes to the small intestine; it consists of pulpy half-digested food, gastric juices and enzymes.

Cilia Microscopic hair-like structures that pulse to move liquids and particles along inside some parts of the body.

Coronary Anything to do with the arteries that supply the heart with blood.

Dairy products Milk and foods that are made from milk, such as butter and cheese.

Dentine The dense material underneath a tooth's outer coating of enamel.

Digestive system The system of tubes that breaks down food and absorbs it into the body.

Embryo The name for a developing baby up to the eighth week.

Enamel The hard and glossy coating on a tooth.

Endocrine system The system that controls the body's internal environment, using chemical messengers called hormones.

Enzyme A protein that speeds up chemical reactions in the body.

Epiglottis A flap of cartilage at the back of the throat that stops food and liquid getting into the lungs.

Foetus A developing baby from the eighth week until birth.

Genes Chemical instructions made of DNA and kept in the nucleus, or control centre, of a cell; they hold information on how to build a human body.

Glucose A sugar that is the body's main energy source.

Gonads The sex organs (male or female).

Hepatic Anything to do with the liver.

Hormone A chemical messenger that carries a signal from one cell to another; hormones are released by glands and cells.

Immune system The defence system that protects the body from infection.

Intercostal muscles Muscles between the ribs that help with breathing.

Lactic acid A mildly toxic waste product made by muscles during heavy exercise (when not enough oxygen is getting to the muscles).

Lobe A rounded body part, which often forms a section of a large organ such as the brain, liver or lungs.

Lymph A clear fluid that surrounds all body cells.

Lymphatic system The body system that drains and transports lymph and works with the immune system to fight infection.

Meninges A series of protective layers surrounding the brain and spinal cord.

Mucus A slimy bodily fluid produced by the linings or coverings of organs.

Musculoskeletal system The load-bearing system that supports the body (skeleton) and pulls on it to move it around (muscles).

Nervous system The network of nerve cells and fibres that transmits information around the body as electrical pulses; made up of the central nervous system (brain and spinal cord) and peripheral nervous system (sensory and motor nerves), as well as the autonomic nervous system, which operates automatic bodily functions.

Neuron A single nerve cell.

Nutrients Vital chemicals we get from food, needed for the body's smooth running and growth.

Osteocyte A bone-making cell.

Proteins A group of essential body chemicals that are used to build new tissues such as muscle fibres, hair and nails; antibodies and enzymes are also proteins.

Pulmonary Anything to do with the lungs.

Renal Anything to do with the kidneys.

Reproductive system The body system that makes sex cells (sperm in males and eggs in females) and takes charge of making new humans.

Respiratory system The system in charge of breathing air, bringing fresh oxygen into the body and releasing waste carbon dioxide.

Sinus A cave-like opening in a bone that can often fill with fluid.

Sphincter A ring of muscle controlling an opening in the body, for example the anus or the bladder's outlet.

Synapse A structure that allows a neuron to pass on an electrical or chemical signal to another cell.

Urea A waste product from the breakdown of proteins in the body; removed in urine (pee).

Urinary system The system that filters waste and excess water from the blood and releases it from the body as urine (pee).

Viruses Tiny infectious agents, usually much smaller than bacteria, that multiply inside cells.

Index